Great Knitted Gifts

Great
Knitted
Gifts

Andrea and Gayle Shackleton

Sterling Publishing Co., Inc. New York
A Sterling/Chapelle Book

Chapelle, Ltd.:
Jo Packham, Sara Toliver, Cindy Stoeckl, Matt DeMaio

Editor: *Leslie Farmer*
Book Design: *Rose Sheifer*
Photography: *Ryne Hazen for Hazen Photography*
Photo Stylist: *Michelle Myers*

If you have any questions or comments, please contact:
Chapelle, Ltd., Inc., P.O. Box 9252, Ogden, UT 84409
(801) 621-2777 • (801) 621-2788 Fax
e-mail: chapelle@chapelleltd.com
Web site: www.chapelleltd.com

Space would not permit the inclusion of every decorative item
photographed for this book, nor could all of the designers be
identified. Many of these items are available by contacting:
Ruby & Begonia, 204 25th Street, Ogden, UT 84401
(801) 334-7829 • (888) 888-7829 Toll-free
e-mail: ruby@rubyandbegonia.com
Web site: www.rubyandbegonia.com

Every effort has been made to ensure that all information in this book is accurate.
However, due to differing conditions, tools, and individual skills, the publisher cannot
be responsible for any injuries, losses, and/or other damages which may result from
the use of the information in this book.

Due to limited amount of available space, we must print our patterns at a reduced
size in order to give our patrons the maximum number of patterns possible in our
publications. We believe the quality and quantity of our patterns will compensate for
any inconvenience this may cause.

This volume is meant to stimulate craft ideas. If readers are unfamiliar or not proficient
in a skill necessary to attempt a project, we urge that they refer to an instructional book
specifically addressing the required technique.

Library of Congress Cataloging-in-Publication Data

Shackleton, Andrea.
Great knitted gifts / Andrea and Gayle Shackleton.
    p. cm.
"Sterling/Chapelle book."
Includes index.
ISBN 1-4027-1323-1
1. Knitting--Patterns. I. Shackleton, Gayle. II. Title.

TT820.S46 2005
746.43'2041--dc22
                                                    2004018223
10 9 8 7 6 5 4 3

Published by Sterling Publishing Co., Inc.
387 Park Avenue South, New York, NY 10016
©2005 by Andrea and Gayle Shackleton
Distributed in Canada by Sterling Publishing
c/o Canadian Manda Group, 165 Dufferin Street
Toronto, Ontario, Canada M6K 3H6
Distributed in the United Kingdom by GMC Distribution Services,
Castle Place, 166 High Street, Lewes, East Sussex,
England BN7 1XU
Distributed in Australia by Capricorn Link (Australia) Pty. Ltd.
P. O. Box 704, Windsor, NSW 2756, Australia
Printed and Bound in China
All Rights Reserved

Sterling ISBN 1-4027-1323-1

For information about custom editions, special sales, premium and
corporate purchases, please contact Sterling Special Sales
Department at 800-805-5489 or specialsales@sterlingpub.com

Table of Contents

Introduction

After 19 years of operating our knitwear company, and designing thousands of sweaters, we are happy to have this opportunity to share some of our favorite patterns. We have selected pieces that range from those that are fun and easy to knit to some that are more challenging. All are perfect for gift-giving.

Great Knitted Gifts is made up of four chapters—each coming from its own source of inspiration. Chapter One reveals our love for circles and dots. Seen in its many simple forms, from rocks on the beach, to apples in a bin, to the ripple a raindrop creates in a puddle, the circle inspires us daily. As one experiments with changing the colors or sizes of the dots in the patterns, the design possibilities seem to be endless.

Chapter Two is one of our favorites. We are both avid gardeners, and when we realized the potential to use flowers—one of our greatest loves—as a design element, we were thrilled. We employed the flower motifs in many ways, from representational to very abstract, and in two- and three-dimensional designs.

In Chapter Three, we explore the possibilities of stripes and squares. The beauty of this chapter's projects is that they are so simple and fun to knit. We encourage you to have a great time knitting and exploring the many color combinations that can be created through the simple technique of striping.

We had a lot of fun with the projects in Chapter Four. We each have two children, who range in age from 3 to 9. Many of these projects were designed with our little ones in mind. You will find the doll clothes are such fun to do for and with your children. The patterns are also a great way to use up all your scrap yarn in a unique and colorful way.

After all these years, we are still passionate about knitting and creating original patterns. We encourage you to play with these patterns, and experiment with the use of color and different yarns. We hope that these projects will bring you and those you give them to as much pleasure as they brought us during the making of this book.

Andrea Shackleton and Gayle Shackleton

Knitting Information

Intarsia

Several pieces in this book are worked using the intarsia method of knitting. Intarsia is a term used to describe a sort of multicolor knitting where you are making blocks of color that stop and are not carried along the full length of the work. Sometimes this is referred to as picture knitting. Small areas such as the polka dots on the Dot Sweater as well as large areas such as the daisy on Ruby's Daisy Sweater can be created using this method.

Each color needs its own bobbin. A bobbin is a length of yarn that is appropriate in length to the area to be knitted. It can be a small ball, a length of yarn wrapped around a small piece of cardboard, or even a single strand of yarn. When handling many yarns of different colors, it is important to keep them organized. One way to do that is to keep your bobbins, or yarn lengths, as short as possible. For example, a tiny dot needs only a few inches of yarn as opposed to a background color that may need a large ball. Simply wind the bobbins necessary for the pattern and work the area of the design with the bobbins rather than the whole ball of yarn as this will be easier to maneuver.

Change yarn colors as directed by the graph, placing the old yarn color over the new yarn color at the back of the knitted piece and continue working. A chain forms on the wrong side of the work where the colors cross. The intarsia method is always worked back and forth. It is never worked in the round. Refer to page 122 for Intarsia detail.

Working with Graphed Patterns

Patterns that call for frequent color changes are often better represented and easier to read when they are charted on a grid.

A graph is made up of individual squares on a grid. Each square represents a stitch. Colors placed within the squares are used to indicate the yarn color used to work the stitch. Each pattern will provide a color key that corresponds with the colors found on the chart. Each horizontal line on the graphed pattern represents a row of knitting.

Start at the bottom right-hand corner of the chart and read to the left. Read the second row from left to right.

It is important to remember that the graphs represent the pattern as viewed on the right side of the knitted fabric. This means that on wrong-side rows (from left to right) you must purl any stitch that would be knitted on the right side rows. At first, this may seem a bit confusing, but as you continue working with the graph, you will soon become accustomed to the method.

Some of the projects in this book are striped patterns which are fun to do in the round on circular needles. You can follow the chart or directions without worrying about whether you have the wrong side or the right side of the knitted fabric facing you.

Note: Many of the knitted items in this book are large articles of clothing and require breaking up the graphed patterns into sections over one or more pages. For ease in working the design, it is recommended that you color-photocopy the sections (enlarging them as desired) and piece them together as one. For the larger designs such as the Dot Sweater, Jesse's Cardigan, and Ruby's Daisy Sweater, a map is also provided at the end of the graphs to help you know how to piece the sections together.

Sample Graphed Pattern

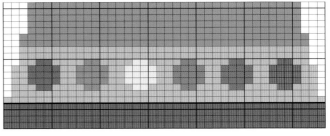

Combination Stitch Patterns

Often a pattern will be a combination of the two formats with some of the instructions written out and some of them graphed. The pattern may include a graph to show a particular stitch color pattern.

Note: Purchase either a line marker or long self-stick notes to help keep track of your place on the chart. Position the marker or note along the row directly above the row that you are currently working. This way you can see where you are in the pattern by comparing the rows you have already worked in your piece to the rows you currently see on the graph.

Pattern Contents

Generally, all sizes and numbers given in the pattern instructions are for the smallest size. Larger sizes, if applicable, are listed in order in parentheses. If only one number is given, it applies to all sizes.

Note: Before you begin knitting, it is a good idea to highlight or circle the size you will be making throughout the pattern to eliminate errors.

Your pattern will tell you what size needles are recommended. It will also tell you how many stitches to cast on and instruct you, row by row, what stitches to use, or it will simply give you one stitch and tell you to knit for a determined number of inches.

The pattern will also tell you when to start forming elements of the project such as armholes, and give you the order for knitting separate pieces of a garment.

Gauge Notation

Your pattern will include a gauge notation (the number of stitches and rows per inch) for the weight of yarn and size of needles required to make the piece. You may use the gauge provided as a guide, but the most reliable thing to do is to knit your own "gauge swatch" with the yarn you have chosen before starting any project. This way you can see if your tension equals the gauge called for in the pattern. Experiment with your own yarn and different sized needles to get the gauge right.

Measure your gauge with a tape measure or a standard gauge ruler to make certain your gauge matches the one listed in the pattern. Any change in the gauge will result in a knitted piece that differs in size from the measurements provided in the pattern.

If you have too many stitches per inch, you are working too tightly. Switch to larger needles. Similarly, if you have too few stitches per inch, you are working too loosely. In this case, you need to switch to smaller needles. Time spent before you begin knitting the piece will be well worth it when you can knit without worries about the finished size of the garment.

Selecting Yarn

The pieces in this book were worked up with a sport-weight handspun wool yarn. Other yarns such as silk, cotton, and wool blends also could be used. Choose colors and yarns that you like and be creative in replacing our color selections with your own. For the intarsia graphs, you will need many colors. The pattern will show up best and be easiest to knit if the yarn is consistent from color to color. Be creative in mixing yarn types and textures, but be certain to mix only yarns that call for the same cleaning techniques to avoid odd shrinkage.

Block and Press Before Sewing

When sewing up a garment, first block and press all the pieces. The yarn used for construction needs to be of the same washability as the garment. Use the mattress stitch to sew up all your seams as this provides the neatest, most professional finish.

How to Iron Woolen Knits

To press out wrinkles in knitted garments, place a damp cloth between the iron and the garment and press on the wrong side of the knit.

Take care

When you give your knitted piece, include the washing instructions, which are found on the yarn label. This helps the receiver know to how to take care of the gift.

Circles
and Dots

Circles Scarf and Hat

CIRCLES SCARF

Materials

YARN

100% wool, handspun, sportweight
- MC – Sand
- CC (A) – Apple
- CC (B) – Bark
- CC (C) – Brown
- CC (D) – Butter
- CC (E) – Celery
- CC (F) – Jute
- CC (G) – Mocha
- CC (H) – Natural
- CC (I) – Sky
- CC (J) – Tan

NOTIONS

Cardboard for making pom-poms

Single-pointed knitting needles, size 4, or size to obtain gauge

MEASUREMENTS

8½" wide x 64" long

GAUGE

6 sts x 8 rows = 1"

STITCH PATTERNS

St st, Seed st

Scarf

- Using spn and MC, CO 51 sts.
- Work in Seed st for 16 rows.
- Work length of scarf in st st, following Circles Scarf Graph on pages 12–13, always starting with 4 Seed sts and ending with 4 Seed sts.
- Work in Seed st for 16 rows.
- BO.

Finishing

- Refer to Pom-pom on page 123. Make six large pom-poms using all the colors.
- Attach three pom-poms onto each end of scarf.

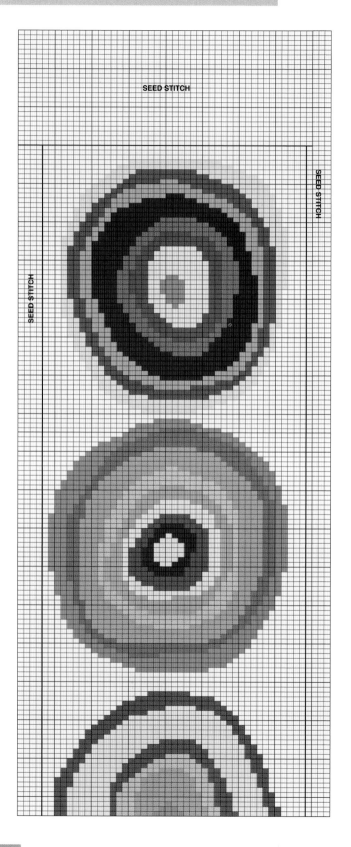

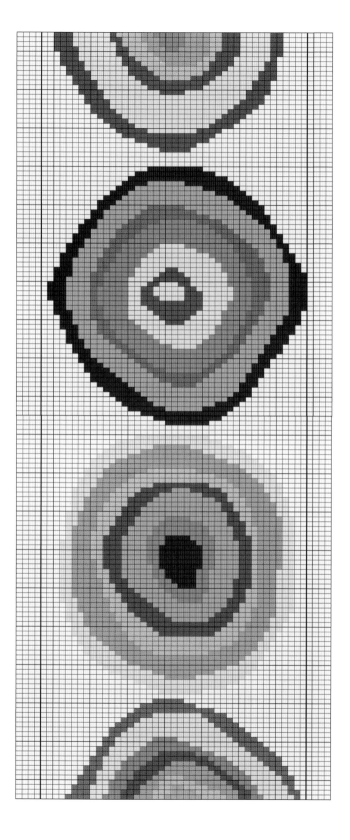

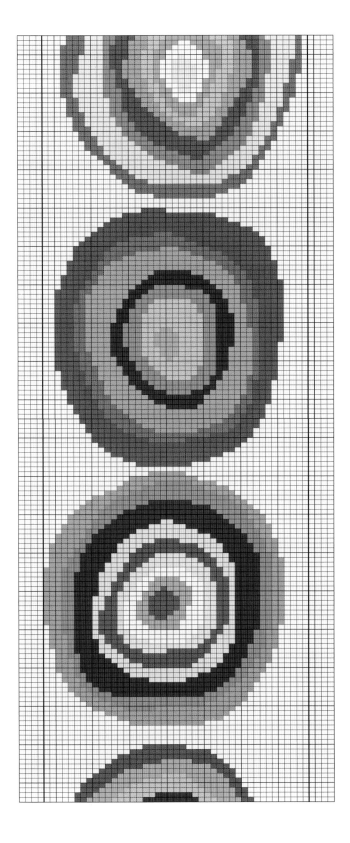

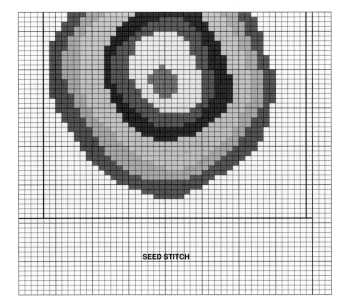

SEED STITCH

Natural		Bark
Sand		Mocha
Butter		Jute
Sky		Tan
Apple		Brown
Celery		

A charming reminder for knitting stitches
Under the fence, catch the sheep;
Back we come, off we leap.

…

Color-photocopy the graph sections. Piece the photocopies together with Section 1 at the top, then Section 2 followed by Section 3, and Section 4 at the bottom. Begin knitting at the bottom-right corner of the graph and work to the left and up. Keep track of rows with a line counter or by covering or crossing out rows that have already been knitted.

CIRCLES HAT

Materials

YARN

100% wool, handspun, sportweight

    MC – Sand

    CC (A) – Apple

    CC (B) – Bark

    CC (C) – Brown

    CC (D) – Butter

    CC (E) – Celery

    CC (F) – Jute

    CC (G) – Mocha

    CC (H) – Natural

    CC (I) – Sky

    CC (J) – Tan

NOTIONS

Cardboard for making pom-pom

Single-pointed knitting needles, size 4, or size to obtain gauge

Yarn needle

MEASUREMENT

approximately 22" around

GAUGE

6 sts x 8 rows = 1"

STITCH PATTERNS

St st, K1P1 ribbing

Hat

- Using spn and MC, CO 142 sts.
- Work in st st for 6 rows.
- Beg K1P1 ribbing on a purl row and work in pattern for 20 rows. This will make the roll turn to the outside when cuffed.
- Work in st st for the next 30 rows, following Circles Hat Graph on pages 15–16.
- On next row, beg decrease. Repeat from ★ to ★.

    Row 1: ★K2tog, k17★ (6 times), k2tog, k18

    Row 2 (and all even rows until Row 18): P

    Row 3: ★K2tog, k16★ (6 times), k2tog, k17

    Row 5: ★K2tog, k15★ (6 times), k2tog, k16

    Row 7: ★K2tog, k14★ (6 times), k2tog, k15

    Row 9: ★K2tog, k13★ (6 times), k2tog, k14

    Row 11: ★K2tog, k12★ (6 times), k2tog, k13

    Row 13: ★K2tog, k11★ (6 times), k2tog, k12

    Row 15: ★K2tog, k10★ (6 times), k2tog, k11

    Row 17: ★K2tog, k9★ (6 times), k2tog, k10

    Row 18: P9, p2tog, ★p8, p2tog★ (6 times)

    Row 19: ★K2tog, k7★ (6 times), k2tog, k8

    Row 20: P7, p2tog, ★p6, p2tog★ (6 times)

    Row 21: ★K2tog, k5★ (6 times), k2tog, k6

    Row 22: P5, p2tog, ★p4, p2tog★ (6 times)

    Row 23: ★k2tog, k3★ (6 times), k2tog, k4

    Row 24: P3, p2tog, ★p2, p2tog★ (6 times)

    Row 25: ★K2tog, k1★ (6 times), k2tog, k2

    Row 26: P1, p2tog, ★p2tog★ (every st to end) until there are 8 sts.

- Using yarn needle, draw these sts tog and tie off inside hat.

Finishing

- Seam back of hat, making certain to seam brim on the reverse side. This is so that when the brim is turned up the seam does not show.
- Refer to Pom-pom on page 123. Make one large pom-pom using all of the colors. Attach to the center top of the hat.

Natural

Sand

Butter

Sky

Apple

Celery

Bark

Mocha

Jute

Tan

Brown

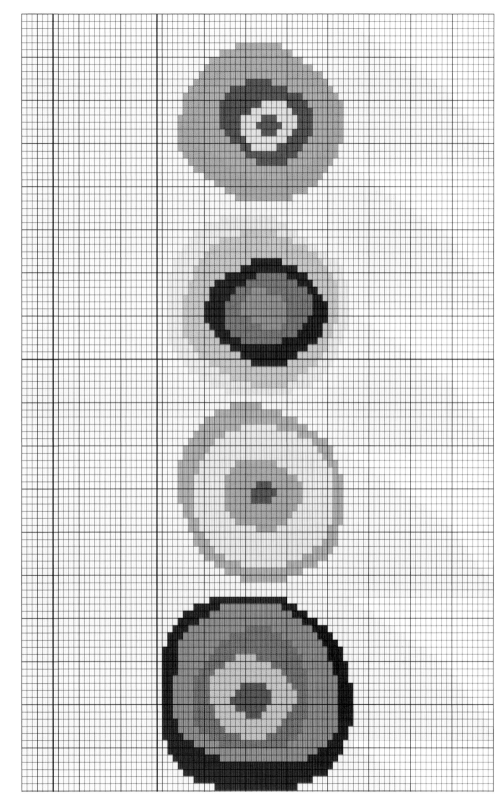

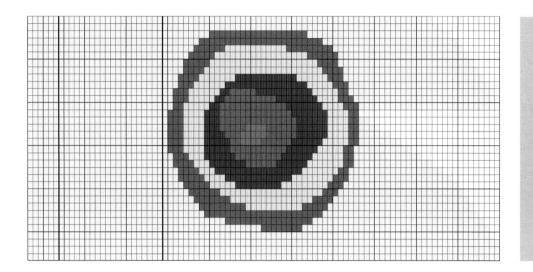

Color-photocopy the graph sections. Piece the photocopies together with Section 1 at the top, and Section 2 at the bottom. Turn the combined graph so that the longer edge is now the bottom edge. Begin knitting at the bottom-right corner of the graph and work to the left and up.

Alternate color scheme
MC – Bark
CC (A) – Apple
CC (B) – Black
CC (C) – Brown
CC (D) – Celery
CC (E) – Charcoal
CC (F) – Jute
CC (G) – Olive
CC (H) – Plum
CC (I) – Rose
CC (J) – Violet

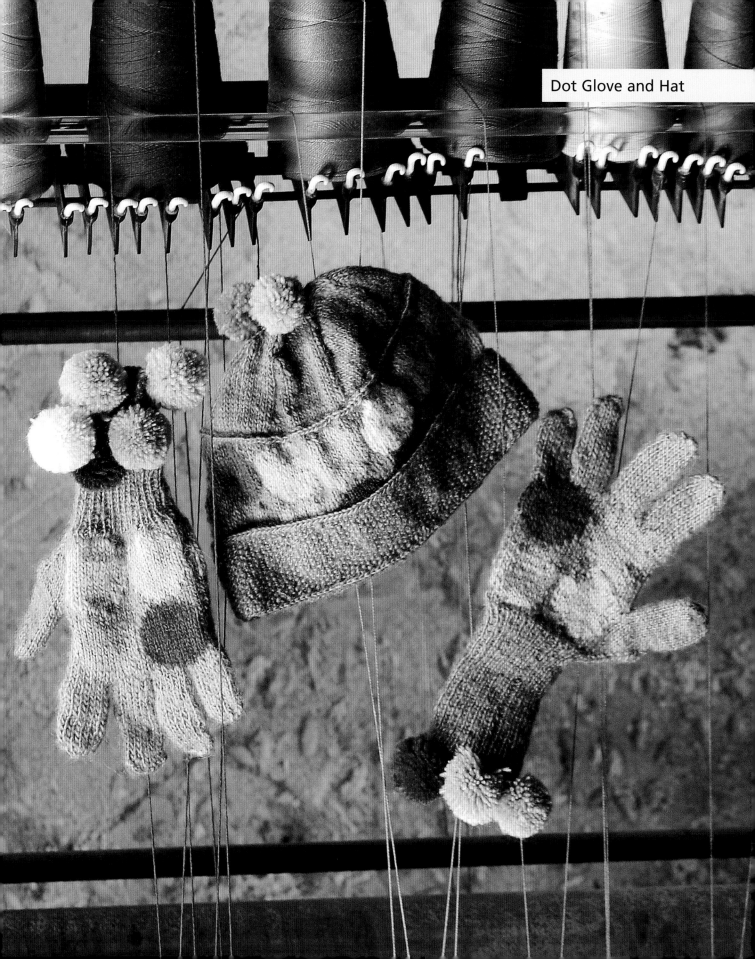

Dot Glove and Hat

DOT GLOVE

Materials

YARN

100% wool, handspun, sportweight

MC - Celery

CC (A) - Apple

CC (B) - Brown

CC (C) - Jute

CC (D) - Mocha

NOTIONS

Cardboard for making pom-poms

Double-pointed knitting needles, size 4

Single-pointed knitting needles, size 4, or size to obtain gauge

Yarn needle

MEASUREMENT

fits woman's hand

GAUGE

6 sts x 8 rows = 1"

STITCH PATTERNS

St st, K1P1 ribbing

Glove Body

- Using spn and MC, CO 50 sts.
- Work in K1P1 ribbing for 40 rows, following the Dot Glove Graph on page 19.
- On next row, work in st st and continue following the graph, increasing 4 sts evenly spaced across row until there are 54 sts.
- On next row, p 1 row.
- Increase 1 st at the beg and 1 st at the end of the row, always increasing 1 st from the end. This creates the thumb gusset.
- Continue in pattern and increasing on either side of the glove every alternate row until there are 68 sts.
- K 5 rows in pattern.
- Break yarn.

Thumb

- Put the first 8 sts on a holder.
- Join MC and k across, following the graph until 8 sts remain.
- Put these 8 sts on a holder. These 16 sts are for the thumb.
- K for 18 rows, following graph until intarsia pattern for dots is completed.
- At this point, fold the glove and seam along the side, leaving an opening for the thumb.

Finger Foundation

- Change to dpn and divide sts evenly on three needles, being careful not to twist sts.
- Mark beg of row. K 2 rows in MC.

Note: Be prepared to work each finger separately on dpn. As each finger will have 12 sts, you must pick up 6 sts from either side of the glove body.

Index Finger

- At the beg of the next rnd, k 6 sts.
- Put 36 sts on a holder and k the next 6 sts.
- You will now have 12 sts to work the index finger.
- Put these 12 sts on 3 dpn, evenly distributed.
- K 21 rows on these 12 sts or until finger measures ½" less than desired length.
- On the next rnd, K2tog all the way around until there are 6 sts.
- On the next rnd, K2tog all the way around until there are 3 sts.
- Using yarn needle, draw these sts tog and bury in the weave.

Middle Finger

- K 6 sts from the beg of sts on holder and 6 sts from the end of sts on holder—you will have 12 sts.
- Divide them evenly on 3 dpn and mark beg of row.
- K 23 rows or until middle finger measures ½" less than desired length.
- On the next rnd, K2tog all the way around until there are 6 sts.
- On the next rnd, K2tog all the way around until there are 3 sts.
- Using yarn needle, draw these sts tog and bury in the weave.

Ring Finger

- K 6 sts from the beg of sts on holder and 6 sts from the end of sts on holder. Work the ring finger in the same manner as index finger.

Pinkie Finger

- K 12 sts rem on holder. Work pinkie in the same manner as index finger, making it 5 rows shorter.

Finishing

- Refer to Pom-pom on page 123. Make 10 small pom-poms in assorted CC yarns and sew onto edge of cuff, evenly spaced.

Dot Glove Graph

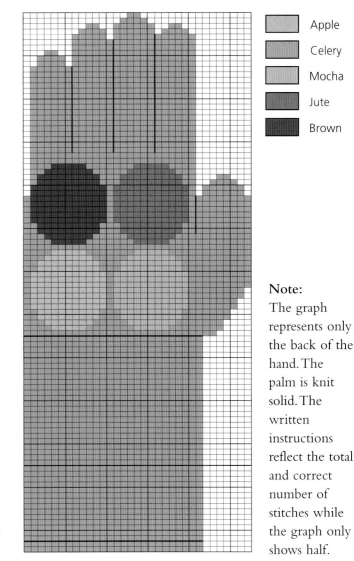

Apple
Celery
Mocha
Jute
Brown

Note:
The graph represents only the back of the hand. The palm is knit solid. The written instructions reflect the total and correct number of stitches while the graph only shows half.

DOT HAT

Materials

YARN

100% wool, handspun, sportweight

    MC - Celery

    CC (A) - Apple

    CC (B) - Bark

    CC (C) - Butter

    CC (D) - Brown

    CC (E) - Jute

    CC (F) - Mocha

    CC (G) - Natural

    CC (H) - Sand

    CC (I) - Sky

    CC (J) - Tan

NOTIONS

Cardboard for making pom-poms

Crochet hook, size E

Single-pointed knitting needles, size 4, or size to obtain gauge

Yarn needle

MEASUREMENT

approximately 24" around

GAUGE

6 sts x 8 rows = 1"

STITCH PATTERNS

St st, Seed st

Hat

- Using spn and MC, CO 146 sts.
- Work in Seed st for 2¼".
- Work in st st for 12 rows.
- Work next 31 rows, following the Dot Hat Graph on pages 21–22.
- K 2 rows.
- Beg decrease, starting on a knit row. Repeat from ★ to ★.

    Row 1: ★K2tog, k19★ (6 times), k2tog, k20

    Row 2 (and all even rows until Row 20): P

    Row 3: K2tog, k19, ★k2tog, k18★ (6 times)

    Row 5: K2tog, k18, ★k2tog, k17★ (6 times)

    Row 7: K2tog, k17, ★k2tog, k16★ (6 times)

    Row 9: K2tog, k16, ★k2tog, k15★ (6 times)

    Row 11: K2tog, k15, ★k2tog, k14★ (6 times)

    Row 13: K2tog, k14, ★k2tog, k13★ (6 times)

    Row 15: K2tog, k13, ★k2tog, k12★ (6 times)

    Row 17: K2tog, k12, ★k2tog, k11★ (6 times)

    Row 19: K2tog, k11, ★k2tog, k10★ (6 times)

    Row 20: ★P9, p2tog★ (6 times), p10, p2tog

    Row 21: K2tog, k9, ★k2tog, k8★ (6 times)

    Row 22: ★P7, p2tog★ (6 times), p8, p2tog

    Row 23: K2tog, k7, ★k2tog, k6★ (6 times)

    Row 24: ★P5, p2tog★ (6 times), p6, p2tog

    Row 25: K2tog, k5, ★k2tog, k4★ (6 times)

    Row 26: ★P3, p2tog★ (6 times), p4, p2tog

    Row 27: K2tog, k3 ★k2tog, k2★ (6 times)

    Row 28: ★P1, p2tog★ (6 times), p2, p2tog

    Row 29: K2tog, k1, ★k2tog★ (every st to end) until there are 8 sts.

- Using yarn needle, draw these sts tog and tie off inside hat.

Finishing

- Seam back of hat, making certain to seam Seed st brim on the reverse side. This is so that when the brim is turned up the seam does not show.
- Refer to Pom-pom on page 123. Make three small pom-poms using three CC yarns. Attach pom-poms onto the top center of the hat.

Crochet Finishing

- Turn Seed st cuff. Using crochet hook and MC, SC 1 row to secure the fold.
- SC 1 row over the CO row.
- SC 1 row around the hat at the point where the decreases start. This makes the pillbox shape.

Dot Hat Graph SECTION 1

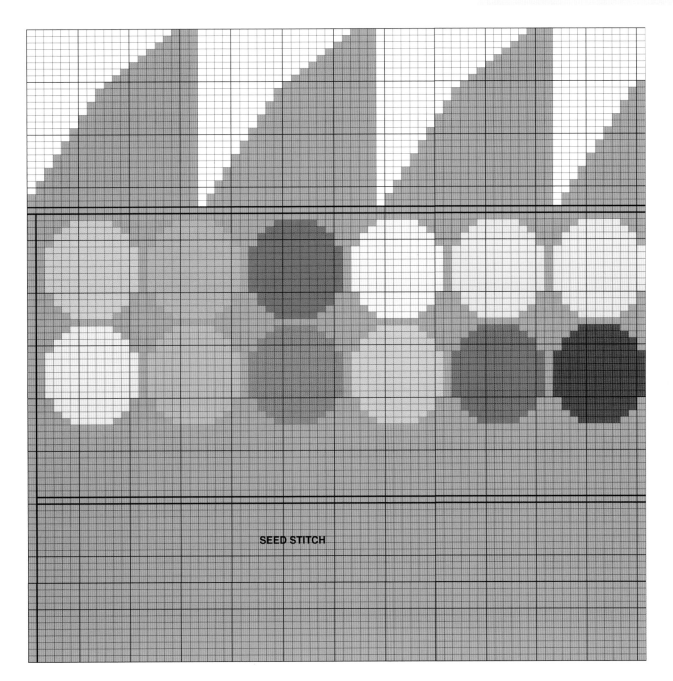

SEED STITCH

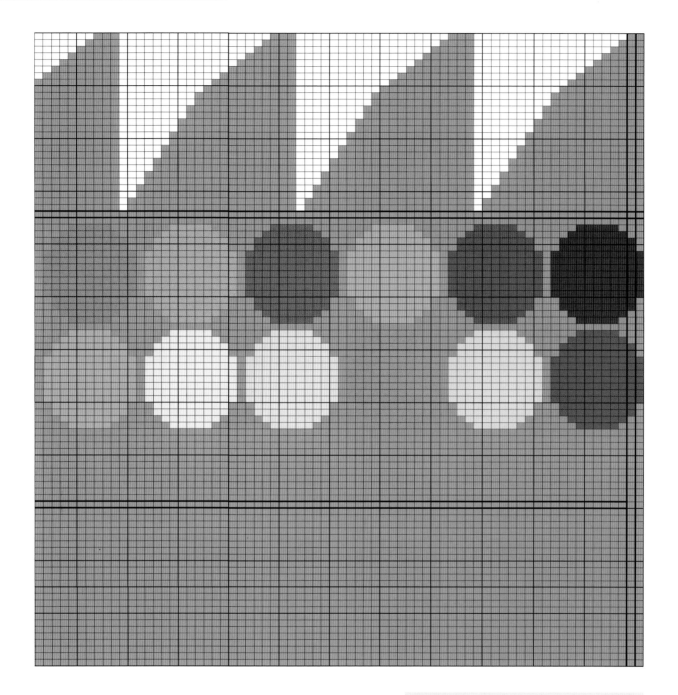

	Natural		Apple		Jute
	Sand		Celery		Tan
	Butter		Bark		Brown
	Sky		Mocha		

Color-photocopy the graph sections. Piece the photocopies together with Section 1 at the left, and Section 2 at the right. Begin knitting at the bottom-right corner of the graph and work to the left and up.

Dot
Sweater

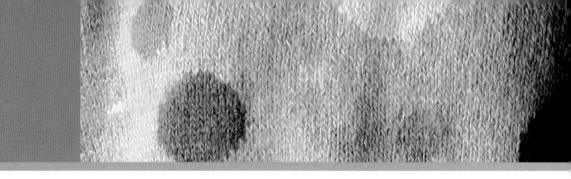

Materials

YARN
100% wool, handspun, sportweight

MC - Sky
CC (A) - Apple
CC (B) - Aqua
CC (C) - Bark
CC (D) - Butter
CC (E) - Creme
CC (F) - Dk. Brown
CC (G) - Fern
CC (H) - Jute
CC (I) - Natural
CC (J) - Olive
CC (K) - Sepia

NOTIONS
Double-pointed knitting needles, size 4, or size to obtain gauge

Single-pointed knitting needles, size 4, or size to obtain gauge

Yarn needle

MEASUREMENTS
Length: 22½"
Chest: 23"
Sleeve: 19½" (from shoulder seam)

GAUGE
6 sts x 8 rows = 1"

STITCH PATTERNS
St st, K1P1 ribbing

Back
- Using spn and MC, CO 138 sts.
- Work in st st for 6 rows.
- Work in K1P1 ribbing for 8 rows.
- Work in st st, following Dot Sweater Graph on pages 25–28 until piece measures 21" from the bottom with the bottom unrolled.
- **Shape back of neck:** Put center 40 sts on a holder.
- Work decreases on each side of the sts on holder (back of neck) every other row four times on neck edge.
- Put rem sts on a holder. There will be 46 sts on each shoulder.

Front
- Work as for back, following the graph until piece measures 17½", from the bottom with the bottom unrolled.
- **Shape neck:** Put center 16 sts on a holder.
- Decrease 1 st on each side of the sts on holder (the neck) every row seven times, every row five times, and every fourth row four times.
- Put rem sts on a holder. There will be 46 sts on each shoulder.
- K front and back shoulders tog from the inside.

Sleeve
- Pick up 114 sts—57 sts on either side of the shoulder seam—by picking up 3 sts, skip 1 all the way along the side, 1 st in from the edge. Begin 9¾" from the shoulder seam.
- Work in st st down to the cuff, following Dot Sweater Sleeve Graph on pages 29–31.
- Decrease every fourth row, 1 st in from edge on both sides, 30 times, as indicated on the graph until pattern is complete and there are 54 sts.
- Using MC, work in K1P1 ribbing for 8 rows.
- Work in st st for 6 rows and BO loosely.

Finishing

- Using the mattress stitch, seam tog by folding sweater at shoulder, stitching up the body and down the sleeve. Make certain to seam on the reverse side for the roll at the bottom and at the cuff.

Neck Finishing

- Using dpn (or a small circular needle), pick up 128 sts.
- Making certain to mark the beg of row, work in K1P1 ribbing for 8 rows.
- Work in st st for 6 rows.
- BO loosely.

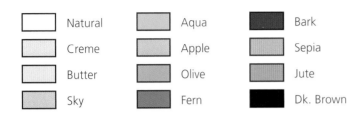

☐	Natural	☐	Aqua	☐	Bark
☐	Creme	☐	Apple	☐	Sepia
☐	Butter	☐	Olive	☐	Jute
☐	Sky	☐	Fern	☐	Dk. Brown

Dot Sweater Graph SECTION 1

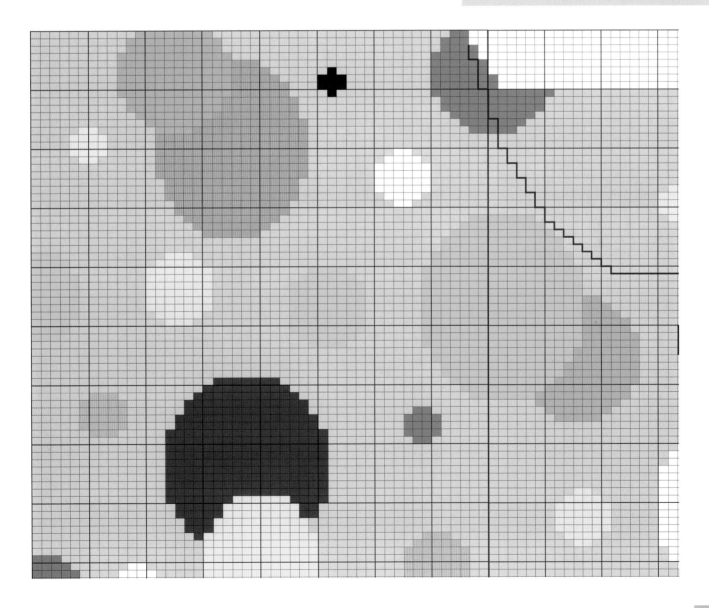

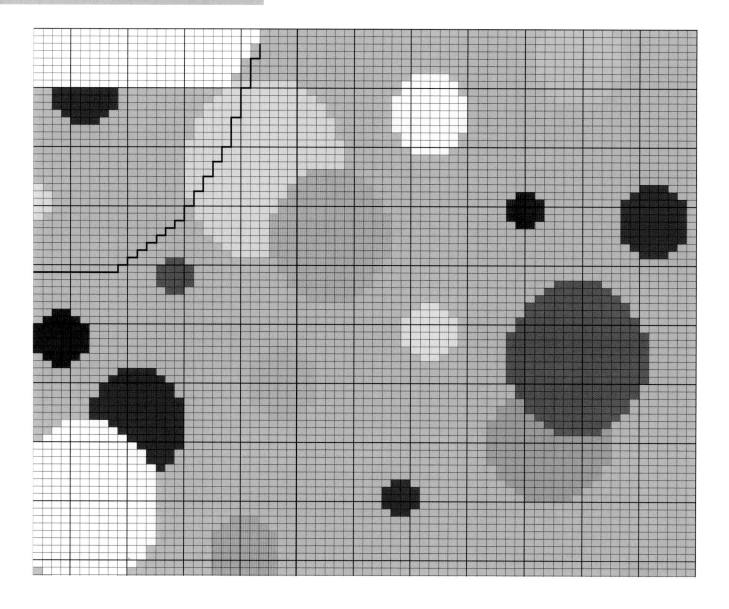

Mattress stitch:

The mattress stitch can be worked either one stitch in from the edge or a half stitch in from the edge, depending on the thickness of the yarn and how neat the edge is.

Make a figure eight: place the two pieces in left hand, without overlapping, and with the two right sides facing you. Pick up the strand between first and second stitches on top piece. Repeat with lower piece. (See diagram at right.)

Repeat, working loosely for two or three stitches, then pull the thread to draw stitches together tightly. Stretch the seam slightly to give it some elasticity, then continue stitching.

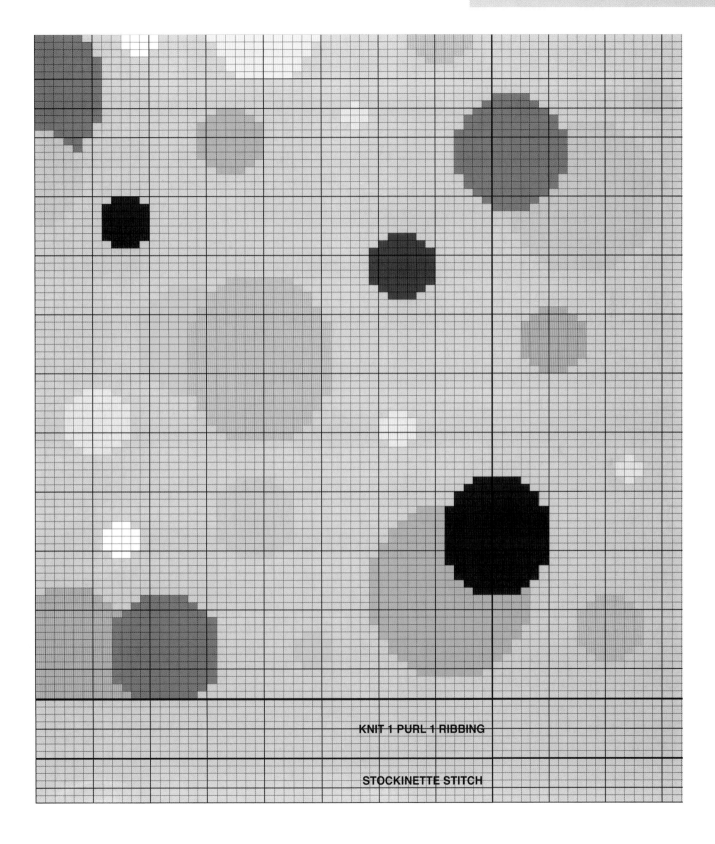

KNIT 1 PURL 1 RIBBING

STOCKINETTE STITCH

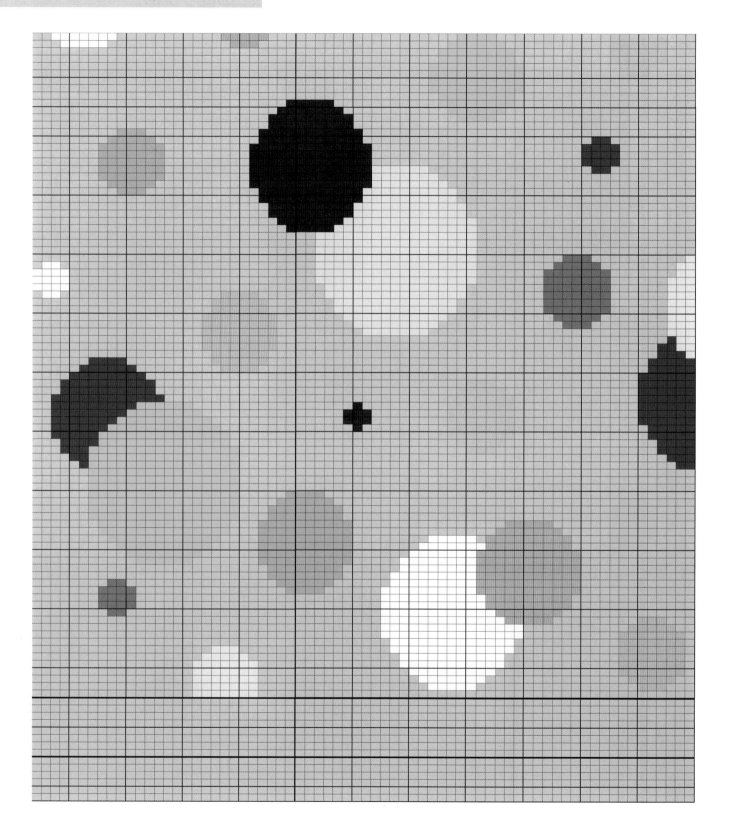

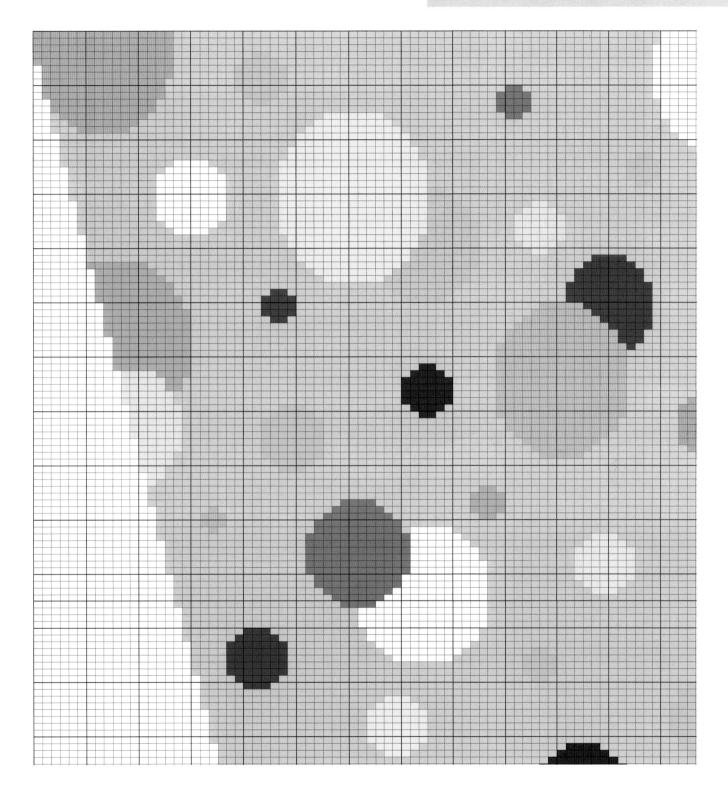

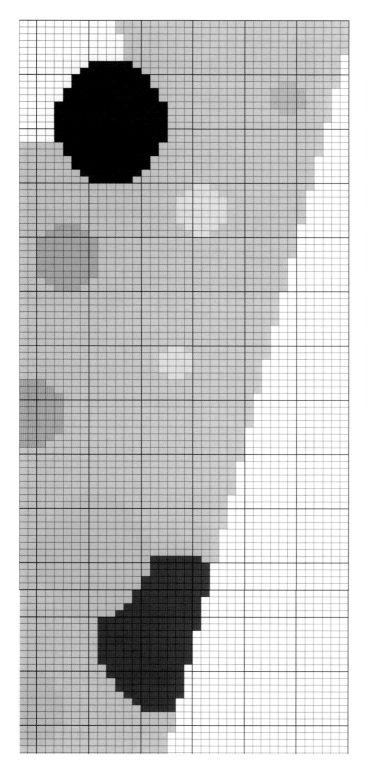

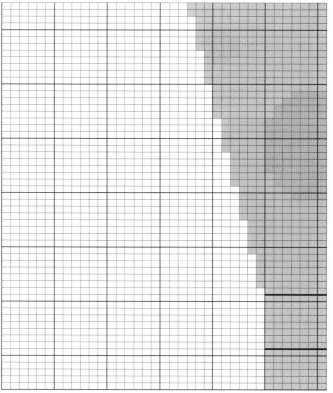

For both the Dot Sweater Graph and the Dot Sweater Sleeve Graph, color-photocopy the graph sections. Piece the photocopies together with Section 1 at the top left, Section 2 at the top right, Section 3 at the bottom left, and Section 4 at the bottom-right. (See Dot Sweater Map and Dot Sweater Sleeve Map on page 31.) Begin knitting at the bottom right corner of the graph and work to the left and up.

. . .

Don't get turned around:
If you put down your work in the middle of a row, you may become disoriented in your knit-ting. When picking up your knitting again, the worked stitches should be on the right-hand needle and the unworked stitches should be on the left-hand needle. The yarn is always attached to the worked stitches.

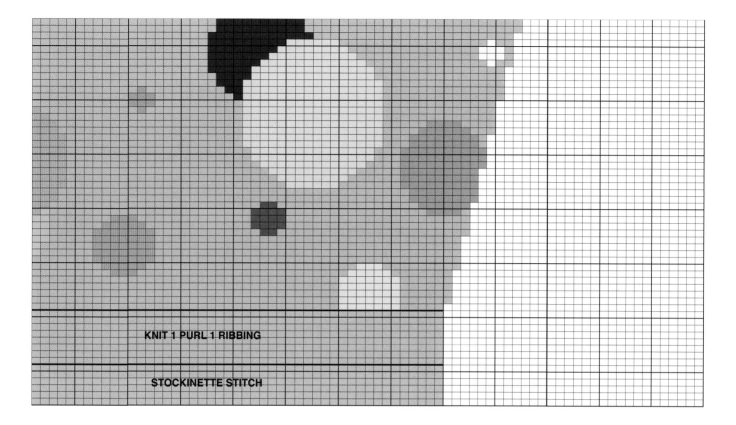

KNIT 1 PURL 1 RIBBING

STOCKINETTE STITCH

Dot Sweater Map

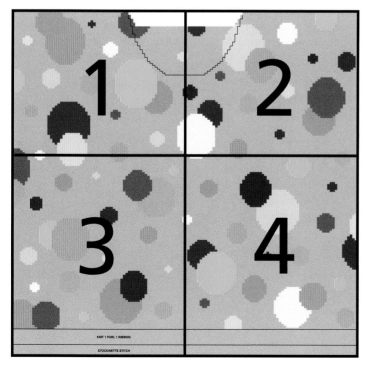

Dot Sweater Sleeve Map

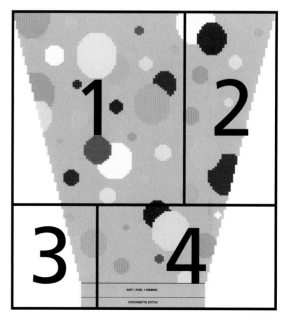

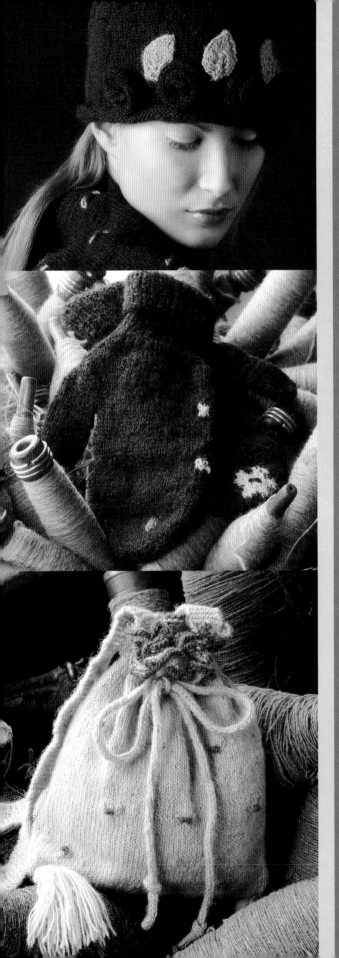

Flowers

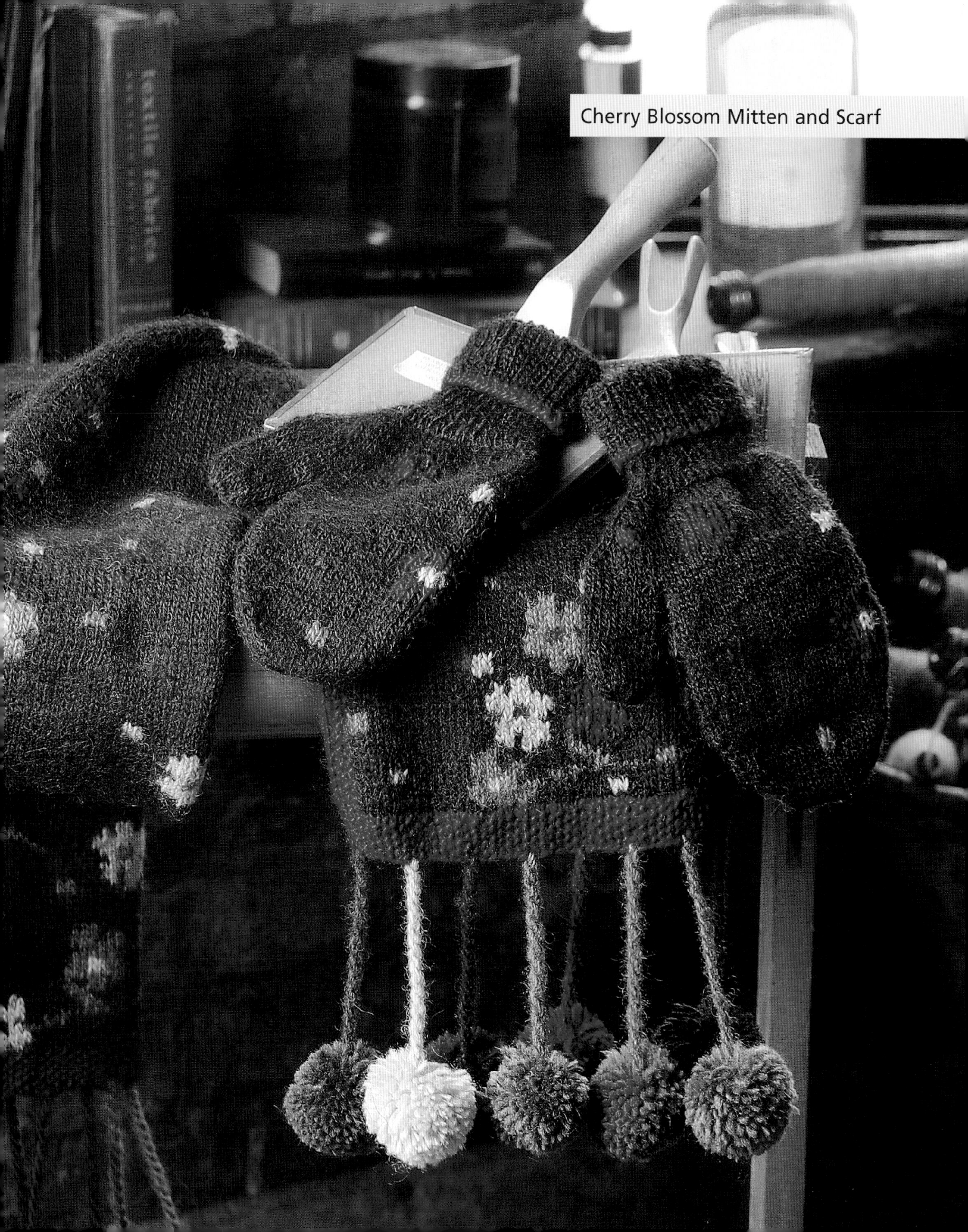

Cherry Blossom Mitten and Scarf

Cherry Blossom Mitten and Scarf

CHERRY BLOSSOM MITTEN

Materials

YARN

100% wool, handspun, sportweight

MC – Burgundy

CC (A) – Mahogany

CC (B) – Raspberry

CC (C) – Red

CC (D) – Rose

NOTIONS

Double-pointed knitting needles, size 4

Single-pointed knitting needles, size 4, or size to obtain gauge

Yarn needle

MEASUREMENT

fits woman's hand

GAUGE

6 sts x 8 rows = 1"

STITCH PATTERNS

St st, K1P1 ribbing

Body of Mitten

- Using spn and color C, CO 50 sts.
- Work 2 rows in K1P1 ribbing.
- Change to MC and work 38 rows in K1P1 ribbing.
- On next row, change to st st, increasing 6 sts evenly spaced across row.

Thumb Gusset

- Continue in st st, following Cherry Blossom Mitten Graph on page 36 and increasing on every other row at the beg and the end of the row until there are 66 sts. Always increase 1 st in from the edge.
- K for 5 rows in pattern.
- Break yarn.

Thumb Opening

- Put the first 8 sts on a holder.
- Join MC and k across, following the graph until 8 sts rem.
- Put these 8 sts on a holder. These 16 sts are for the thumb.
- Work in pattern for 30 rows, ending with a purl row.

Top of Mitten

- Continue in pattern and beg decrease, or shaping, for the top of the mitten.

  Row 1: K1, skp, k20, k2tog, skp, k20, k2tog, k1
  Row 2 (and all even rows until Row 12): P
  Row 3: K1, skp, k18, k2tog, skp, k18, k2tog, k1
  Row 5: K1, skp, k16, k2tog, skp, k16 ,k2tog, k1
  Row 7: K1, skp, k14, k2tog, skp, k14, k2tog, k1
  Row 9: K1, skp, k12, k2tog, skp, k12, k2tog, k1
  Row 11: K1, skp, k10, k2tog, skp, k10, k2tog, k1
  Row 12: P1, p2tog, p8, p2tog, p2tog, p8, p2tog, p1
  Row 13: K1, skp, k6, k2tog, skp k6, k2tog, k1
  Row 14: P1, p2tog, p4, p2tog, p2tog, p4, p2tog, p1
  Row 15: K1, skp, k2, k2tog, skp, k2, k2tog, k1

  until there are 10 sts.
- Refer to Kitchener Stitch on page 122. At this point, fold mitten in half and use Kitchener st to connect 5 sts to 5 sts on either side of mitten.
- Seam mitten tog, leaving the hole for the thumb open.

Thumb

- Using dpn and MC, divide 16 sts on holder evenly on three needles, making certain not to twist sts in round.
- Mark beg.
- K for 12 rows.
- Beg decrease, or shaping, for thumb:

  Row 1: K2tog, k2tog, k8, k2tog, k2tog
  Row 2: K
  Row 3: K2tog, k2tog, k4, k2tog, k2tog
  Row 4: K2tog all the way around until there are 4 sts.
- Using yarn needle, draw these sts tog and tuck in all ends.

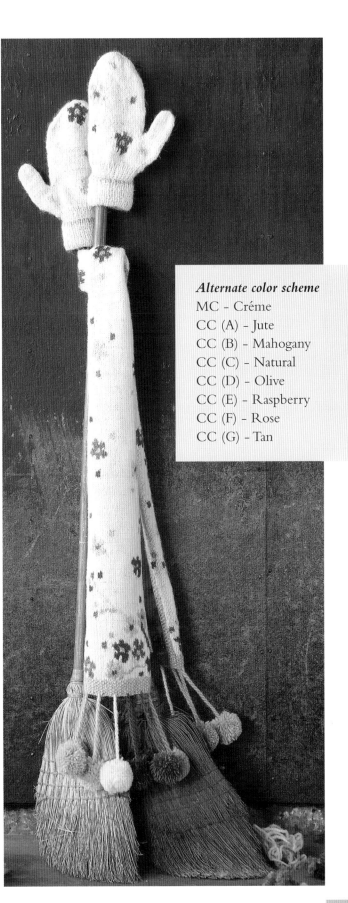

Alternate color scheme
MC – Créme
CC (A) – Jute
CC (B) – Mahogany
CC (C) – Natural
CC (D) – Olive
CC (E) – Raspberry
CC (F) – Rose
CC (G) – Tan

Cherry Blossom Mitten Graph

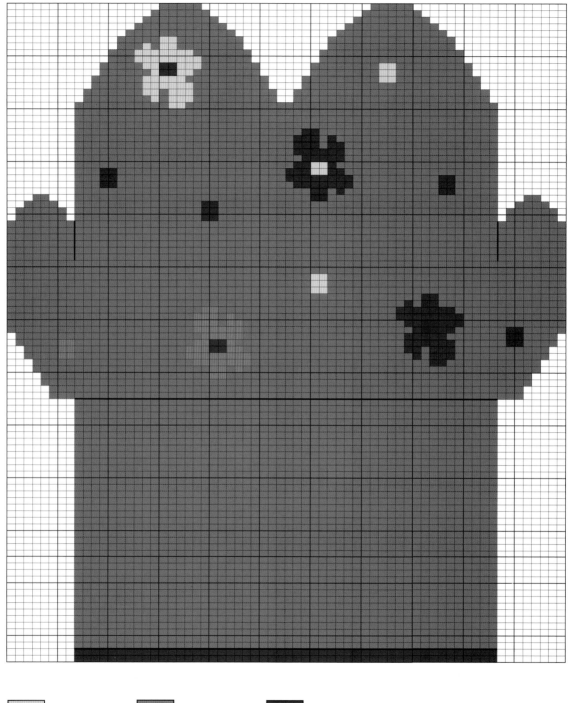

Rose	Raspberry	Mahogony
Red	Burgundy	

CHERRY BLOSSOM SCARF

Materials

YARN

100% wool, handspun, sportweight

MC - Burgundy
CC (A) - Dk Green
CC (B) - Mahogany
CC (C) - Olive
CC (D) - Pine
CC (E) - Raspberry
CC (F) - Red
CC (G) - Rose

NOTIONS

Cardboard for making
pom-poms

Single-pointed knitting needles,
size 4, or size to obtain gauge

Yarn needle

MEASUREMENTS

8" wide x 64" long

GAUGE

6 sts x 8 rows = 1"

STITCH PATTERNS

St st, Seed stitch

Scarf

- Using spn and color F, CO 52 sts.
- Work in Seed st for 8 rows.
- Work length of scarf in st st, following Cherry Blossom Scarf Graph on pages 38–39, always starting with 4 sts of Seed st in color F and ending with 4 sts of Seed st in color F.
- Work in Seed st in color F for 8 rows.
- BO.

Finishing

- Refer to Pom-pom on page 123. Make 16 large pom-poms, two in each color.
- Make 16 twisted strings, two in each color. For each, cut two strands 40" long. Fold in half, making four strands. Attach strands at even intervals onto each end of scarf by threading one end of four strands midway through the Seed st band. Each strand will measure approximately 10" before twisting.
- In the folded end, place a pencil or crochet hook and begin twisting.
- Twist the entire strand tightly; it should twist both sides of entire length evenly. Allow the two sides to twist onto themselves. Knot together.
- Attach the pom-pom in the matching color at the knotted end.
- Trim ends.

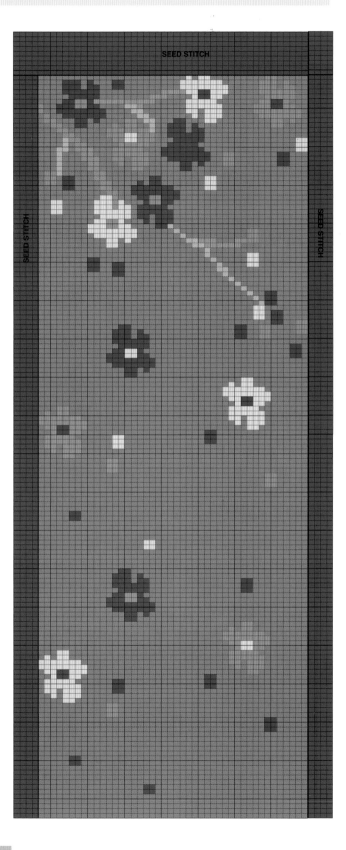

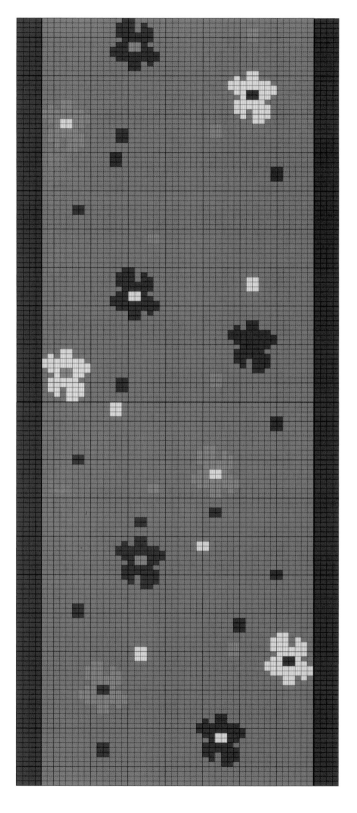

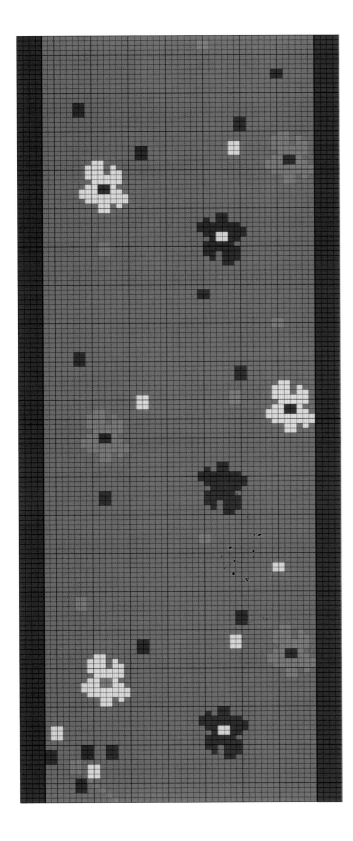

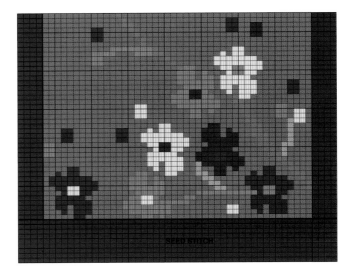

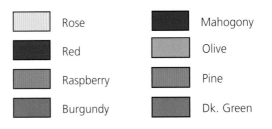

	Rose		Mahogony
	Red		Olive
	Raspberry		Pine
	Burgundy		Dk. Green

Color-photocopy the graph sections on these two pages. Piece the photocopies together with Section 1 at the top, then Section 2 followed by Section 3, and Section 4 at the bottom. Begin knitting at the bottom-right corner of the graph and work to the left and up.

…

Yarn storage

If you will not be using the yarn for a while, store it as a skein, not as a ball since wool can be stretched out when it is stored as a ball. Before you begin knitting, however, it is helpful to unwind any skeins and wind the yarn into balls. Keep your yarns clean and separated by placing each in its own container.

Ruffle-edged Glove, Pillbox Hat, and Drawstring Bag

RUFFLE-EDGED GLOVE

Materials

YARN

100% wool, handspun, sportweight
MC - Crème
CC (A) - Rose
CC (B) - Sage

NOTIONS

Double-pointed knitting needles, size 4

Single-pointed knitting needles, size 4, or size to obtain gauge

Yarn needle

MEASUREMENT

fits woman's hand

GAUGE

6 sts x 8 rows = 1"

STITCH PATTERNS

St st, K1P1 ribbing

Glove Body

- Using spn and color A, CO 200 sts.
- Change to MC and k2tog across row until there are 100 sts.
- On next row, p2tog across row until there are 50 sts.
- Work in st st for 2 rows.
- Work in K1P1 ribbing for 20 rows.
- On next row, change to st st, increasing 4 sts evenly spaced across row until there are 54 sts.
- On next row, p 1 row.
- Increase 1 st at the beg and 1 st at the end of the row, always increasing 1 st from the end. This creates the thumb gusset.
- Continue increasing on either side of the glove every alternate row until there are 68 sts.
- K for 5 rows.
- Break yarn.

Thumb

- Put the first 8 sts on a holder.
- Join MC and k across until 8 sts remain.
- Put these 8 sts on a holder. These 16 sts are for the thumb.
- K for 18 rows.
- At this point, fold the glove and seam along the side, leaving an opening for the thumb.

Finger Foundation

- Change to dpn and divide sts evenly on three needles, being careful not to twist sts.
- Mark beg of row. K 2 rows in MC.

Note: Be prepared to work each finger separately on dpn. As each finger will have 12 sts, you must pick up 6 sts from either side of the glove body.

Index Finger

- At the beg of the next rnd, k 6 sts.
- Put 36 sts on a holder and k the next 6 sts.
- You will now have 12 sts to work the index finger.
- Put these 12 sts on 3 dpn, evenly distributed.
- K 21 rows on these 12 sts or until finger measures ½" less than desired length.
- On the next rnd, k2tog all the way around until there are 6 sts.
- On the next rnd, k2tog all the way around until there are 3 sts.
- Using yarn needle, draw these sts tog and bury in the weave.

Middle Finger

- K 6 sts from the beg of sts on holder and 6 sts from the end of sts on holder—you will have 12 sts.
- Divide them evenly on 3 dpn and mark beg of row.
- K 23 rows or until middle finger measures ½" less than desired length.
- On the next rnd, k2tog all the way around until there are 6 sts.
- On the next rnd, k2tog all the way around until there are 3 sts.
- Using yarn needle, draw these sts tog and bury in the weave.

Ring Finger

- K 6 sts from the beg of sts on holder and 6 sts from the end of sts on holder. Work the ring finger in the same manner as index finger.

Pinkie Finger

- K 12 sts rem on holder. Work pinkie in the same manner as index finger, making it 5 rows shorter.

Embroidery Finishing

- Using a yarn needle and waste yarn, mark flower placement at every 10 sts, alternating placement every 10 rows or where desired—embroider roses on the back of the hand only.
- Refer to Bullion Rose on page 122. Make bullion roses in color A at each marking.
- Refer to Lazy Daisy on page 123. Make lazy daisy leaves in color B on the sides of each rose.

Clever holders and markers

Instead of purchasing expensive stitch holders and markers, look around to see how you can use everyday items to accomplish the task. A double-pointed needle can hold a small number of stitches. Different sizes of safety pins also work well for holding stitches.

When marking a stitch, you can use twist-ties, pieces cut from plastic drinking straws, scraps of yarn, or tiny rubber bands that can be found in the hair-care products section at discount stores. All of these are available in multiple colors and make marking your place quick and inexpensive.

RUFFLE-EDGED PILLBOX HAT

Materials

YARN
100% wool, handspun, sportweight
- MC - Crème
- CC (A) - Rose
- CC (B) - Sage

NOTIONS
Crochet hook size E

Single-pointed knitting needles, size 4, or size to obtain gauge (you may need a circular needle because of the large amount of sts needed to create the ruffle edging)

Yarn needle

MEASUREMENT
approximately 22" around

GAUGE
6 sts x 8 rows = 1"

STITCH PATTERNS
St st, K1P1 ribbing

Ruffle Edge

- Using spn and color A, CO 568 sts.
- Change to MC and k2tog across row until there are 284 sts.
- On next row, p2tog across row until there are 142 sts.
- Work in st st for 5 rows.
- On next row (a purl row—you will turn this small brim up after the hat is finished), work in K1P1 ribbing for 5 rows.

Hat Body

- Work in st st for 5¼".
- Beg decreases on a knit row:
  - Row 1: ★K2tog, k17★ (6 times), k2tog, k18
  - Row 2 (and all even rows until Row 18): P
  - Row 3: ★K2tog, k16★ (6 times), k2tog, k17
  - Row 5: ★K2tog, k15★ (6 times), k2tog, k16
  - Row 7: ★K2tog, k14★ (6 times), k2tog, k15
  - Row 9: ★K2tog, k13★ (6 times), k2tog, k14
  - Row 11: ★K2tog, k12★ (6 times), k2tog, k13
  - Row 13: ★K2tog, k11★ (6 times), k2tog, k12
  - Row 15: ★K2tog, k10★ (6 times), k2tog, k11
  - Row 17: ★K2tog, k9★ (6 times), k2tog, k10
  - Row 18: P9, p2tog, ★p8, p2tog★ (6 times)
  - Row 19: ★K2tog, k7★ (6 times), k2tog, k8
  - Row 20: P7, p2tog, ★p6, p2tog★ (6 times)
  - Row 21: ★K2tog, k5★ (6 times), k2tog, k6
  - Row 22: P5, p2tog, ★p4, p2tog★ (6 times)
  - Row 23: ★K2tog, k3★ (6 times), k2tog, k4
  - Row 24: P3, p2tog, ★p2, p2tog★ (6 times)
  - Row 25: ★K2tog, k1★ (6 times), k2tog, k2
  - Row 26: P1, p2tog, ★p2tog ★ (every st to end) until there are 8 sts.
- Using yarn needle, draw these sts tog and tie off inside hat.

Finishing

- Seam back of hat, making certain to seam small brim through K1P1 ribbing on the reverse side. This is so that when the brim is turned up the seam does not show.

Crochet Finishing

- Turn brim at ribbing. Using crochet hook and MC, SC 1 row to secure the fold.
- SC 1 row at the point where the decreases start. This will create the pillbox shape.

- For crochet loops at the top, attach MC to the center top of the hat and chain 10, then attach remaining end. Repeat for three loops.

Embroidery Finishing

- Using a darning needle and waste yarn, mark flower placement at every 20 sts, alternating placement every 10 rows or where desired.
- Refer to Bullion Rose on page 122. Make bullion roses in color A at each marking.
- Refer to Lazy Daisy on page 123. Make lazy daisy leaves in color B on the sides of each rose.

RUFFLE-EDGED DRAWSTRING BAG

Materials

YARN
100% wool, handspun, sportweight
  MC - Crème
  CC (A) - Rose
  CC (B) - Sage

NOTIONS
Double-pointed knitting needles, size 4 for knitted cord

Single-pointed knitting needles, size 4, or size to obtain gauge

Yarn needle

MEASUREMENT
10" square (without strap)

GAUGE
6 sts x 8 rows = 1"

STITCH PATTERNS
St st, Garter st

Sides A & B

- Using spn and color A, CO 240 sts.
- Change to MC and k2tog across row until there are 120 sts.
- On next row, p2tog across row until there are 60 sts.
- Work in st st until piece measures 10" from beg.
- BO.
- Repeat all for side B.

Strap

- Using spn and MC, CO 7 sts.
- Work in garter st until strap measures 45".
- BO.

Knitted Cord

- Using dpn and MC, CO 3 sts.
- ★K3★ Do not turn work, slide sts to right end of needle. Pull yarn to tighten. Repeat from ★ to ★ until cord measures 34".
- Finish by k all 3 sts tog and pulling yarn through last st.

Construction

- Seam Side A and Side B along the bottom and both sides.

- Sew strap onto the inside of the bag, 1" down, at the side seams.
- Thread knitted cord through weave, 2" down from the top. Starting 5 sts from the center front of the bag, going over and under approximately 5 sts at a time, ending 5 sts away from where you started.
- Using yarn needle, draw these sts tog and weave in the ends.

Embroidery Finishing

- Using a yarn needle and waste yarn, mark flower placement at every 20 sts, alternating placement every 20 rows or where desired.
- Refer to Bullion Rose on page 122. Make bullion roses in color A at each marking.
- Refer to Lazy Daisy on page 123. Make lazy daisy leaves in color B on the sides of each rose.

Tassel Finishing

- Refer to Tassel on page 124. Make two tassels.
- Attach one to each bottom corner of bag.

Alternate color scheme
MC - Silver
CC (A) - Rose
CC (B) - Gray

Rose Hat and Scarf

ROSE HAT

Materials

YARN

100% wool, handspun,
sportweight

MC - Black

CC (A) - Burgundy

CC (B) - Olive

NOTIONS

Single-pointed knitting needles,
size 4, or size to obtain gauge

Yarn needle

MEASUREMENT

approximately 22" around

GAUGE

6 sts x 8 rows = 1"

STITCH PATTERN

St st

Hat

- Using spn and MC, CO 142 sts.
- Work in st st for 5½".
- On a knit row, beg decreases:

    Row 1: ★K2tog, k17★ (6 times), k2tog, k18

    Row 2 (and all even rows until Row 18): P

    Row 3: ★K2tog, k16★ (6 times), k2tog, k17

    Row 5: ★K2tog, k15★ (6 times), k2tog, k16

    Row 7: ★K2tog, k14★ (6 times), k2tog, k15

    Row 9: ★K2tog, k13★ (6 times), k2tog, k14

    Row 11: ★K2tog, k12★ (6 times), k2tog, k13

    Row 13: ★K2tog, k11★ (6 times), k2tog, k12

    Row 15: ★K2tog, k10★ (6 times), k2tog, k11

    Row 17: ★K2tog, k9★ (6 times), k2tog, k10

    Row 18: P9, p2tog, ★p8, p2tog★ (6 times)

    Row 19: ★K2tog, k7★ (6 times), k2tog, k8

    Row 20: P7, p2tog, ★p6, p2tog★ (6 times)

    Row 21: ★K2tog, k5★ (6 times), k2tog, k6

    Row 22: P5, p2tog, ★p4, p2tog★ (6 times)

    Row 23: ★K2tog, k3★ (6 times), k2tog, k4

    Row 24: P3, p2tog, ★p2, p2tog★ (6 times)

    Row 25: ★K2tog, k1★ (6 times), k2tog, k2

    Row 26: P1, ★p2tog★ (every st to end) until there are 8 sts.

- Using yarn needle, draw these sts tog and tie off inside hat.

Knitted Roses Finishing

- Refer to Knitted Rose on page 123. Make five roses.
- Sew roses, evenly spaced, onto the hat, 2½" up from the edge of the brim, flattening them as you sew.

Knitted Leaves Finishing

- Refer to Knitted Leaf on page 123. Make four leaves.
- Sew the leaves onto the hat between the roses.

Scarf

- Using spn and MC, CO 56 sts.
- Work in Seed st for 6 rows.
- Work length of scarf in st st until it measures 59½", always starting with 4 Seed sts and ending with 4 Seed sts.
- Work in Seed st for 6 rows.
- BO.

Embroidery Finishing

- Using yarn needle and waste yarn, mark rose placement at every 20 sts, alternating placement every 20 rows or where desired.
- Refer to Bullion Rose on page 122. Make bullion roses in color A at each marking.
- Refer to Lazy Daisy on page 123. Make lazy daisy leaves in color B on the sides of each rose.

ROSE SCARF

Materials

YARN

100% wool, handspun, sportweight

MC - Black

CC (A) - Burgundy

CC (B) - Olive

NOTIONS

Single-pointed knitting needles, size 4, or size to obtain gauge

Yarn needle

MEASUREMENTS

9½" wide x 60" long

GAUGE

6 sts x 8 rows = 1"

STITCH PATTERNS

St st, Seed st

Knitted Roses Finishing

- Refer to Knitted Rose on page 123. Make six roses.
- Sew three roses onto each end of the scarf, flattening them as you sew.

Knitted Leaves Finishing

- Refer to Knitted Leaf on page 123. Make four leaves.
- Sew two leaves onto each end of the scarf, between the roses.

Corkscrew Fringe Finishing

- Refer to Corkscrew Fringe on page 122. Make 12 pieces of corkscrew fringe.
- Attach six pieces of corkscrew fringe onto each end of the scarf at regular intervals.

Squares
and Stripes

Big Squares Knee Sock

Materials

YARN

100% wool, handspun, sportweight

MC - Brick
CC (A) - Bark
CC (B) - Black
CC (C) - Burgundy
CC (D) - Charcoal
CC (E) - Dk Brown
CC (F) - Red
CC (G) - Sepia
CC (H) - Silver

NOTIONS

Double-pointed knitting needles, size 4

Single-pointed knitting needles, size 4, or size to obtain gauge

Yarn needle

MEASUREMENT

fits women's foot sizes 6–9

GAUGE

6 sts x 8 rows = 1"

STITCH PATTERNS

St st, K1P1 ribbing

Sock

- Using spn and MC, CO 80 sts.
- Work in st st for 8 rows.
- Work in K1P1 ribbing for 24 rows.
- Work in st st, following the Big Squares Knee Sock Graph on pages 52–53 until design is complete.
- **Shape calf:** While following the graph, decrease on every seventh row on both sides to shape the calf.

Heel

- Change to dpn.
- Decrease 6 sts evenly spaced across the next row until there are 44 sts.
- **Heel flap:** P11, sl rem sts to next needle. This needle will hold the instep sts. Turn, using empty dpn, k11, then k11 from next needle, sl rem sts to instep needle so there are 22 sts each on two dpn.
- Work back and forth on these 22 sts for 24 rows as follows: ★Sl 1, k1.★ Repeat from ★ to ★, turn. End with a WS row.
- **Turn heel:** Work short rows as follows:
  Row 1: P13, p2tog, p1
  Row 2: Sl 1, k5, k2tog, k1
  Row 3: Sl 1, p6, p2tog, p1
  Row 4: Sl 1, k7, k2tog, k1
  Row 5: Sl 1, p8, p2tog, p1
  Row 6: Sl 1, k9, k2tog, k1
  Row 7: Sl 1, p10, p2tog, p1
  Row 8: Sl 1, k11, k2tog, k1 = 14 heel sts.

Gusset

- Using empty dpn (needle 1), p7. P7 more sts and then pick up and k 14 sts along edge of heel flap. Using needle 2, p22 sts for instep; using needle 3, pick up and k 14 sts along other edge of heel flap and p7 rem sts until there are 64 sts—21 sts each on needles 1 and 3, 22 sts on needle 2.

- Beg rnd at center of heel:

    Rnd 1: P

    Rnd 2: P to last 3 sts of needle 1, p2tog tbl, p1; p22 sts of needle 2; p1, p2tog, p to end of needle 3.

- Repeat Rnds 1 and 2 until 44 sts remain.

Foot

- Work even on dpn in st st until foot measures 8" from back to heel or about 1½" less then desired length.
- Arrange sts so there are 11 sts each on needles 1 and 3, and 22 sts on needle 2.
- **Shape toe:**

    Rnd 1: K

    Rnd 2: K to last 3 sts of needle 1, k2tog tbl, k1; k1, k2tog, k to last 3 sts of needle 2, k2tog tbl, k1; k1, k2tog, p to end of needle 3.

- Repeat Rnds 1 and 2 until there are 20 sts.
- K5 sts from needle 1 onto needle 3 so there are 10 sts each on two dpn.
- Refer to Kitchener Stitch on page 122. Use the Kitchener st to attach the two sides.

Stronger socks

Reinforce the heel on your sock by adding quilter's thread into the weave. This will help keep the stitches from separating and wearing unevenly, cutting down on time spent mending and darning. Use the same technique for the ball of the foot near the toe.

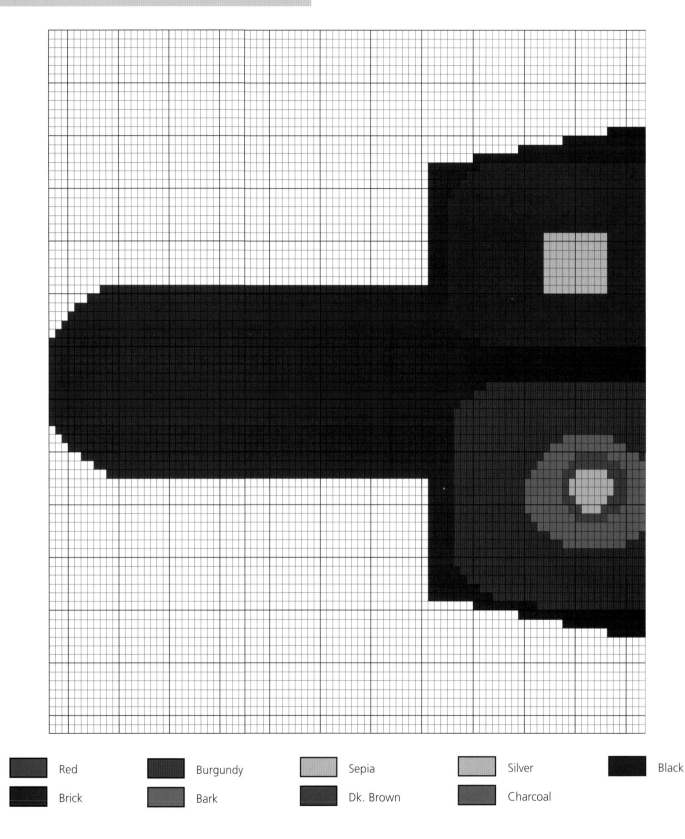

Red	Burgundy	Sepia	Silver	Black
Brick	Bark	Dk. Brown	Charcoal	

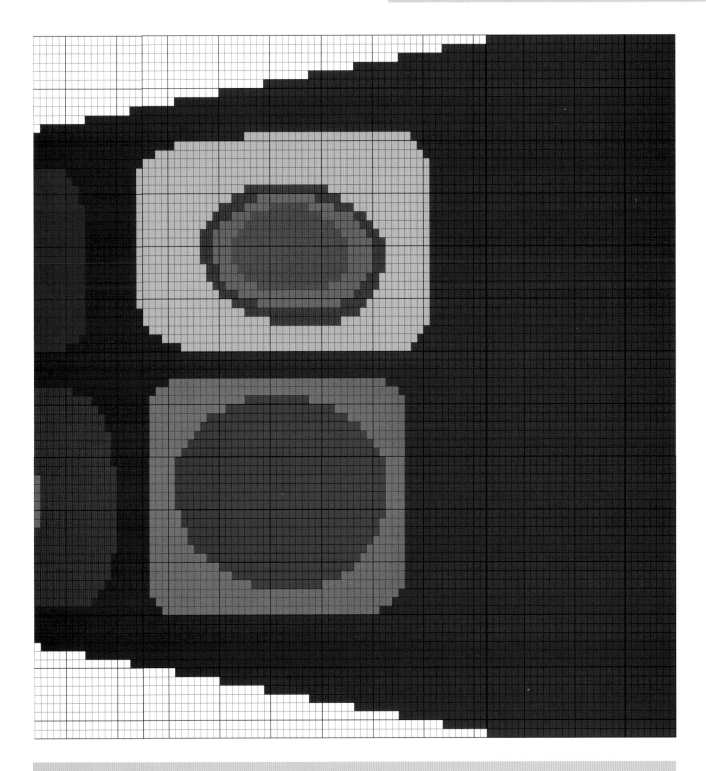

Color-photocopy the graph sections. Piece the photocopies together with Section 1 at the left, and Section 2 at the right. Turn the combined graph so that the right edge of Section 2 is now the bottom edge. Begin knitting at the bottom-right corner of the graph and work to the left and up.

Painted Flower Fingerless Mitten, Hat, and Scarf

PAINTED FLOWER FINGERLESS MITTEN

Materials

YARN

100% wool, handspun, sportweight
Variegated

NOTIONS

Double-pointed knitting needles,
size 4, or size to obtain gauge

Yarn needle

MEASUREMENT

fits woman's hand

GAUGE

6 sts x 8 rows = 1"

STITCH PATTERN

St st

Body of Mitten

- Using dpn, CO 46 sts and divide sts evenly on three needles, making certain not to twist sts.
- Mark beg.
- *P for 4 rows. K for 4 rows. * Repeat from * to * four times.
- P for 4 rows.
- Increase 10 sts evenly across the next row.

Thumb Gusset

- Row 1: K1, then increase and k to within 1 st of the end and increase, k1
- Row 2: K
- Repeat Rows 1 and 2 five times until there are 66 sts, creating the thumb gusset.
- K 5 rows.
- On next row, k 8 sts. Put these 8 sts on a holder. K 50 sts until 8 sts rem. Put these 8 sts on a holder. These 16 sts are for the thumb.
- Redistribute the 50 sts evenly on three needles.
- K for 14 rows.
- BO loosely.

Thumb

- Using dpn, divide 16 sts on holder evenly on three needles, making certain not to twist sts.
- Mark beg.
- K for 7 rows.
- BO loosely.

Creative Yarn Suggestions

- Use up old scraps or collect an exciting mixture of yarns especially for this project. Tie together any kind and length of yarn as long as the weight is consistent. Make a large ball before you start. Tuck in the ends as you knit. The appearance will change dramatically with any number of combinations. Be creative and have fun with texture and color and create your own yarn.

PAINTED FLOWER HAT

Materials

YARN
100% wool, handspun, sportweight
Variegated

NOTIONS
Crochet hook, size E

Single-pointed knitting needles, size 4, or size to obtain gauge

Yarn needle

MEASUREMENT
approximately 22" around

GAUGE
6 sts x 8 rows = 1"

STITCH PATTERN
St st

Hat

- Using spn, CO 142 sts.
- Work in st st for 48 rows.
- On a knit row, beg decreases:

  Row 1: ★K2tog, k17★ (6 times), k2tog, k18
  Row 2 (and all even rows until Row 18): P
  Row 3: ★K2tog, k16★ (6 times), k2tog, k17
  Row 5: ★K2tog, k15★ (6 times), k2tog, k16
  Row 7: ★K2tog, k14★ (6 times), k2tog, k15
  Row 9: ★K2tog, k13★ (6 times), k2tog, k14
  Row 11: ★K2tog, k12★ (6 times), k2tog, k13
  Row 13: ★K2tog, k11★ (6 times), k2tog, k12
  Row 15: ★K2tog, k10★ (6 times), k2tog, k11
  Row 17: ★K2tog, k9★ (6 times), k2tog, k10
  Row 18: P9, p2tog, ★p8, p2tog★ (6 times)
  Row 19: ★K2tog, k7★ (6 times), k2tog, k8
  Row 20: P7, p2tog, ★p6, p2tog★ (6 times)
  Row 21: ★K2tog, k5★ (6 times), k2tog, k6
  Row 22: P5, p2tog, ★p4, p2tog★ (6 times)
  Row 23: ★K2tog, k3★ (6 times), k2tog, k4
  Row 24: P3, p2tog, ★p2, p2tog★ (6 times)
  Row 25: ★K2tog, k1★ (6 times), k2tog, k2
  Row 26: P1, ★p2tog★ (every st to end) until there are 8 sts.

- Using yarn needle, draw these sts tog and tie off inside hat.

Finishing

- Seam back of hat, making certain to seam small brim through first 8 rows on the reverse side. This is so that when the brim is turned up the seam does not show.

Crocheted Flower Finishing

- Refer to Crocheted Flower on page 122. Make one flower.
- Sew flower onto side of hat with center of flower 4" from the edge of brim.

Corkscrew Fringe Finishing

- Refer to Corkscrew Fringe on page 122. Make five pieces of corkscrew fringe.
- Attach three pieces of corkscrew fringe onto the center top of the hat.
- Attach two pieces under the crocheted flower so that they look like vines springing from the side.

PAINTED FLOWER SCARF

Materials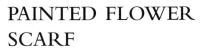

YARN
100% wool, handspun, sportweight
Variegated

NOTIONS
Crochet hook, size E

Single-pointed knitting needles, size 4, or size to obtain gauge

Yarn needle

MEASUREMENTS
8" wide x 66" long

GAUGE
6 sts x 8 rows = 1"

STITCH PATTERNS
St st, Reverse st st

Scarf

◉ Using spn, CO 46 sts.
◉ Work in st st for 6 rows.
◉ *Reverse, work in st st for 4 rows. Reverse, work in st st for 4 rows.* Repeat from * to * three times.
◉ * Work in st st for 8 rows. Reverse, work in st st for 4 rows.* Repeat from * to * until work measures 63" from the beg, or until desired length.
◉ *Reverse, work in st st for 4 rows. Reverse, work in st st for 4 rows.* Repeat from * to * three times.
◉ BO.

Note: In order to Reverse st st:
◉ K 2 rows.
◉ Beg regular st st (k the RS, p the WS).

Crocheted Flower Finishing

◉ Refer to Crocheted Flower on page 122. Make two flowers.
◉ Sew one flower onto each end of the scarf.

Corkscrew Fringe Finishing

◉ Refer to Corkscrew Fringe on page 122. Make 12 pieces of corkscrew fringe.
◉ Attach six pieces of corkscrew fringe onto each end of the scarf at regular intervals.

Pablo Bag

Materials

YARN

100% wool, handspun, sportweight

    CC (A) - Bark

    CC (B) - Brick

    CC (C) - Brown

    CC (D) - Celery

    CC (E) - Dk Brown

    CC (F) - Dk Green

    CC (G) - Gold

    CC (H) - Jute

    CC (I) - Khaki

    CC (J) - Pine

    CC (K) - Tan

NOTIONS

Crochet hook, size E

Single-pointed knitting needles, size 4, or size to obtain gauge

Yarn needle

MEASUREMENTS

10½" wide x 12" long (without strap)

GAUGE

6 sts x 8 rows = 1"

STITCH PATTERNS

St st, Seed st

Bag Body—Front, Back, and Bottom Gusset

- Using spn, CO 56 sts.
- Work in Seed st for 6 rows, following the Pablo Bag Graph on pages 60–61.
- Work in st st, following the graph until you reach the bottom gusset section.
- Work in Seed st to complete the stripes of the bottom gusset section.
- Resume working in st st, following the graph and finish with 6 rows of Seed st as shown on the graph.

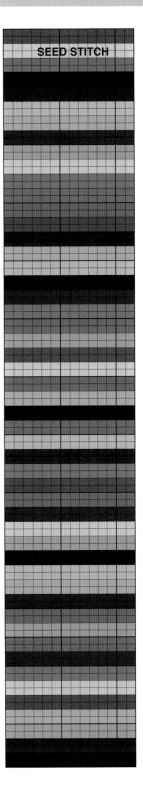

Side Gusset

- Using spn and following Pablo Bag Gusset Graph, CO 14 sts for gusset.
- Work in Seed st for 6 rows.
- Work in st st, following the graph for stripes for remaining gusset rows.
- BO.
- Repeat for two gusset pieces.

Strap

- Using spn, CO 18 sts.
- Work in st st for 23".
- BO.
- Fold in half, making certain that the seam is on the inside of the strap. Using crochet hook, complete 1 row of SC along each side to secure the fold.
- Repeat for two strap pieces.

Finishing

- Fold in half, front to back of bag.
- Sew one gusset onto each side with top, Seed st border, matching the border at the top of bag.
- Sew straps onto top of bag, one in the front and one in the back, 1" down from the top with the seam of the strap to the inside of the bag. The straps should be sewn close to the side gussets, with a 4" span across center front.

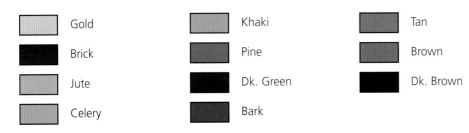

▨ Gold		▨ Khaki		▨ Tan	
▨ Brick		▨ Pine		▨ Brown	
▨ Jute		▨ Dk. Green		▨ Dk. Brown	
▨ Celery		▨ Bark			

Color-photocopy the graph sections on pages 60–61. Piece the photocopies together with Section 1 at the top, and Section 2 at the bottom. Begin knitting at the bottom-right corner of the graph and work to the left and up. To help you keep your place in the design, mark off each row on the graph as it is completed.

SEED STITCH

SEED STITCH

SEED STITCH

Ribbed Market Bag

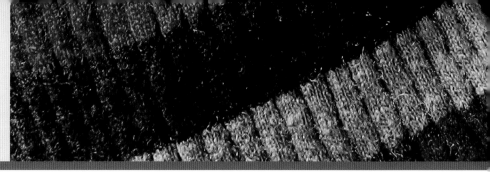

Materials

YARN

100% wool, handspun, sportweight

CC (A) - Black

CC (B) - Brick

CC (C) - Charcoal

CC (D) - Dk Brown

CC (E) - Mahogany

CC (F) - Rust

CC (G) - Tan

NOTIONS

Single-pointed knitting needles, size 4, or size to obtain gauge

Yarn needle

MEASUREMENTS

13" wide x 12" long (without strap)

GAUGE

6 sts x 8 rows = 1"

STITCH PATTERN

K4P2 ribbing

Side A

- Using spn, CO 134 sts.
- Work in K4P2 ribbing as follows:

    Row 1: K3, ★p2, k4★ until 5 sts rem, p2, k3.

    Row 2: P3, ★k2, p4★ until 5 sts rem, p2, k3.

    Repeat Rows 1 and 2, changing colors every 20 rows, following Ribbed Market Bag Graph on pages 65–67 until you have completed seven stripes, or approximately 17".

Side B

- Repeat as for side A.

Strap

- Using spn, CO 28 sts

    Row 1: ★K4, p2★ until 4 sts rem, k4

    Row 2: ★P4, k2★ until 4 sts rem, p4.

- Repeat Rows 1 and 2, changing color every 20 rows until you have completed 20 stripes—approximately 52" or desired length.
- **Strap end shaping:** On the final stripe, make a pointed end by working a decrease on every other row on both sides in pattern until 4 sts rem. Always decrease 1 st in from the edge. On the right side, skp and on left side, k2tog. On the second to last decrease, k2tog two times. On the final decrease, k2tog and pull the strand through the last st.
- Secure end.

Loop

- Using spn, CO 8 sts.
    Row 1: K3, p2, k3
    Row 2: P3, k2, p3.
- Using the color of the first stripe of side A, repeat Rows 1 and 2 for 40 rows (approximately 5" long).
- BO.

Finishing

- Seam Side A and Side B along the bottom and both sides.

- Turn seam to the inside, 30 rows from the top. This is where the bag will cuff over the top.
- Cuff by folding top of bag one and one-half stripes down from the top (30 rows).
- Sew flat end of strap onto the inside of cuff, 1" down, against the side seam on one side.
- On the other side seam, attach the loop by sewing it 1" down inside of the cuff on both sides of the seam.
- Thread the pointed end of the strap through the loop and knot at the desired length.

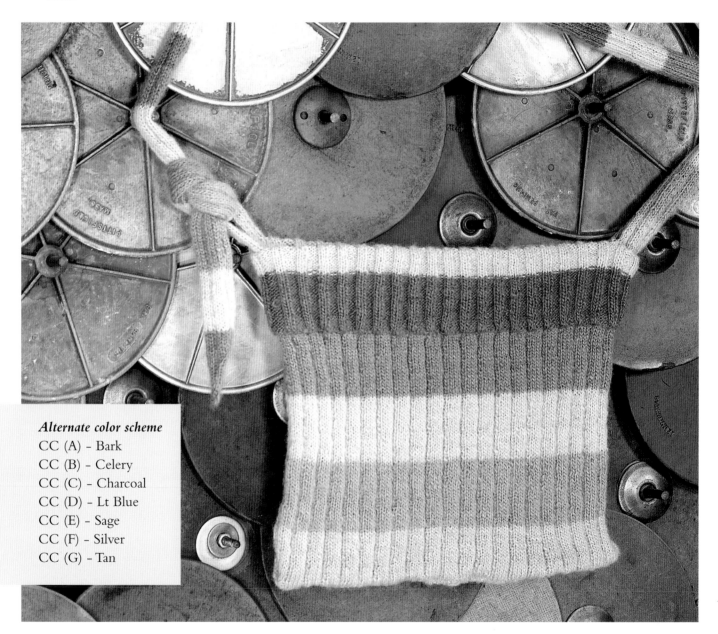

Alternate color scheme
CC (A) - Bark
CC (B) - Celery
CC (C) - Charcoal
CC (D) - Lt Blue
CC (E) - Sage
CC (F) - Silver
CC (G) - Tan

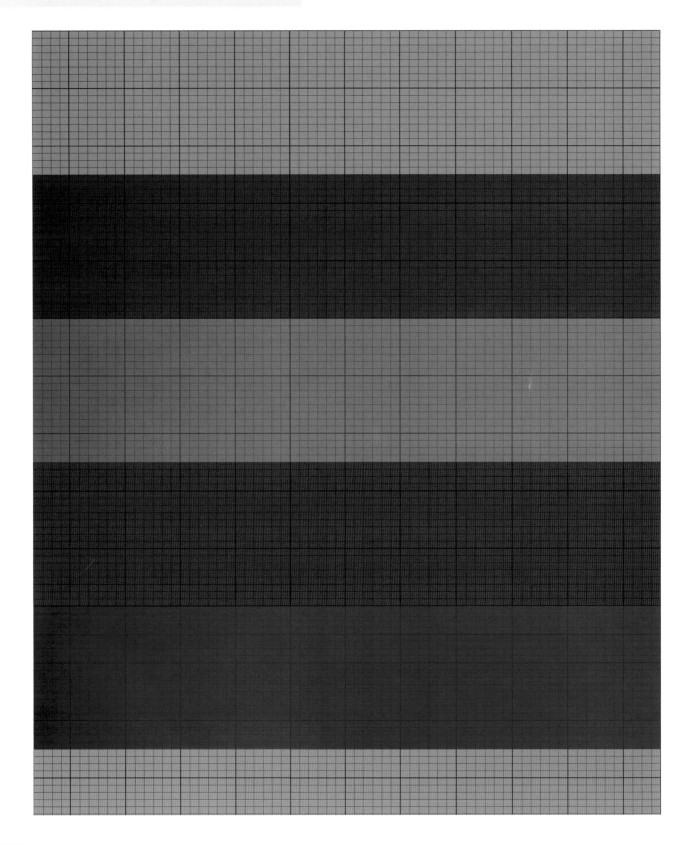

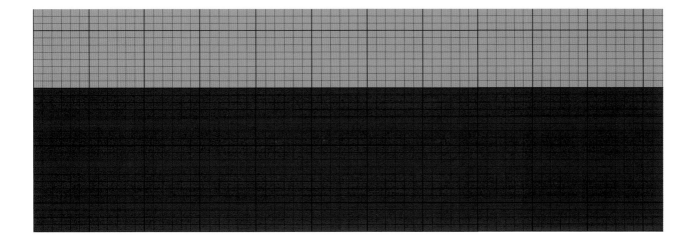

Ribbed Market Bag Graph SECTION 4

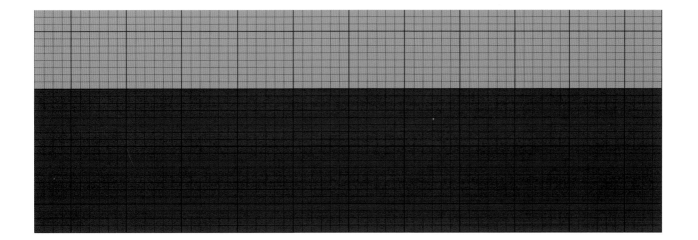

Brick

Rust

Mahogany

Tan

Dk. Brown

Charcoal

Black

Color-photocopy the graph sections on pages 65–67. Piece the photocopies together with Section 1 at the top left, Section 2 at the top right, Section 3 at the bottom left, and Section 4 at the bottom right. Begin knitting at the bottom-right corner of the graph and work to the left and up.

. . .

Twisted stitches:

A stitch is shaped like and upside down U. The right side of the stitch always goes on the front side of the needle and the left side is always on the back. If it is the other way around, your stitch is twisted.

Ribbed Scarf and Hat

RIBBED SCARF

Materials

YARN

100% wool, handspun, sportweight

    CC (A) - Black

    CC (B) - Brick

    CC (C) - Charcoal

    CC (D) - Dk Brown

    CC (E) - Mahogany

    CC (F) - Poppy

    CC (G) - Rose

    CC (H) - Rust

    CC (I) - Tan

NOTIONS

Single-pointed knitting needles, size 4, or size to obtain gauge

Yarn needle

MEASUREMENTS

10" wide x 80" long (without tassels)

GAUGE

7.5 sts x 8 rows = 1"

STITCH PATTERN

K4P2 ribbing

Scarf

- Using spn, CO 76 sts.
- Work in Ribbing Pattern as follows:

    Row 1: K4, ★p2k4★, repeat ★ to ★

    Row 2: P4, ★k2p4★, repeat ★ to ★.

    Repeat Rows 1 and 2, changing colors every 20 rows until you have completed 32 stripes (approximately 80"–90").

Finishing

- Refer to Tassel on page 124. Make 10 tassels of different colors.
- Attach five tassels, evenly spaced, to each end of the scarf.

RIBBED HAT

Materials

YARN

100% wool, handspun, sportweight

    CC (A) - Black

    CC (B) - Brick

    CC (C) - Charcoal

    CC (D) - Mahogany

    CC (E) - Rust

    CC (F) - Tan

NOTIONS

Cardboard for making pom-pom

Single-pointed knitting needles, size 4, or size to obtain gauge

Yarn needle

MEASUREMENT

Approximately 20" around (relaxed)

GAUGE

7.5 sts x 8 rows = 1"

STITCH PATTERN

K4P2 ribbing

Tidy ends:

Remember to tie knots sparingly in your knitting. A knot is usually the first place to wear a hole. Leave ends long enough so they can be woven into the work for an inch or more in opposite directions.

Hat

- Using spn, CO 182 sts.
- Work in Ribbing Pattern as follows:

    Row 1: K1, *p2k4*, repeat * to * until 7 sts remain then, p2k5

    Row 2: P5K2, *p4k2*, repeat * to * until 1 st remains then, p1.

    Repeat rows 1 and 2, changing colors every 15 rows until you have completed four stripes.

- On the next row, beg decreases:

    Row 1: K1, *k2tog, k18* (8 times), k2tog, k19

    Row 2 (and all even rows until Row 20): Purl

    Row 3: K1, *K2tog, K17* (8 times), K2tog, K18

    Row 5: K1, *K2tog, K16* (8 times), K2tog, K17

    Row 7: K1, *K2tog, K15* (8 times), K2tog, K16

    Row 9: K1, *K2tog, K14* (8 times), K2tog, K15

    Row 11: K1, *K2tog, K13* (8 times), K2tog, K14

    Row 13: K1, *K2tog, K12* (8 times), K2tog, K13

    Row 15: K1, *K2tog, K11* (8 times), K2tog, K12

    Row 17: K1, *K2tog, K10* (8 times), K2tog, K11

    Row 19: K1, *K2tog, K9* (8 times), K2tog, K10

    Row 20: P9, P2tog *P8, P2tog* (8 times), P1

    Row 21: K1, *K2tog, K7* (8 times), K2tog, K8

    Row 22: P7, P2tog *P6, P2tog* (8 times), P1

    Row 23: K1, *K2tog, K5* (8 times), K2tog, K6

    Row 24: P5, P2tog *P4, P2tog* (8 times), P1

    Row 25: K1, *K2tog, K3* (8 times), K2tog, K4

    Row 26: P3, P2tog *P2, P2tog* (8 times), P1

    Row 27: K1, *K2tog, K1* (8 times), K2tog, K2

    Row 28: P1, *p2tog* (every st to end) until there are 12 sts.

- Using yarn needle, draw these sts tog and tie off inside hat.

Finishing

- Seam hat, making certain to seam cuff halfway on the reverse side. This is so that when the cuff is turned up the seam does not show.

- Refer to Pom-pom on page 123. Make one large pom-pom using all of the colors. Attach to the center top of the hat.

Alternate color scheme
CC (A) – Bark
CC (B) – Celery
CC (C) – Charcoal
CC (D) – Grape
CC (E) – Lt Blue
CC (F) – Purple
CC (G) – Sage
CC (H) – Silver
CC (I) – Tan

Kids and Holidays

Clothesline Garland

Materials

YARN

100% wool, handspun, sportweight
Any number of colors
(see graphs)

NOTIONS

Baby buttons

Crochet hook, size E

Double-pointed knitting needles,
size 4

Single-pointed knitting needles,
size 4, or size to obtain gauge

Yarn needle

MEASUREMENT

tiny

GAUGE

6 sts x 8 rows = 1"

STITCH PATTERNS

St st, K1P1 ribbing

Our clothesline garland has three Wee Striped Cardigans, two Wee Dot Jumpers, two Wee Striped Socks, three Wee Dot Socks, and two Wee Dot Hats. Use any or all of these to make up your own combinations and create a unique garland.

These tiny articles of clothing will fit small dolls or make interesting ornaments. They make a charming wall decoration in the laundry room and a sweet window treatment in a little girl's room.

They are also a great way to sharpen your knitting skills without requiring a lot of time or yarn. Use up scraps and odd pieces of yarn. Experiment with the colors and patterns and have fun!

WEE SOCK

Sock

- Using spn and color of choice, CO 22 sts loosely.
- Work in st st, following Wee Dot Sock Graph or Wee Striped Sock Graph below, until sock measures 1¾".
- Change to dpn, dividing sts evenly on three needles, and connect sts taking care not to twist them.
- K 2 rnds before beg shaping (continue in stripe pattern if making a striped sock).
- **Divide for heel:** Place 5 sts on each of two needles for top of foot, and 10 sts on the rem needle for the heel flap. If the small size of the sock makes working the heel difficult, place the foot sts on a holder or string to keep them out of the way.
- **Heel flap:** Work in st st for ½", ending with a right side row.
- **Turn heel:**

    Row 1: P to center of heel flap, p next 2 sts tog, p1, turn

    Row 2: Sl 1, k1, ssk, k1, turn

Row 3: Sl 1, p2, p2tog, p1, turn

Row 4: Sl 1, k3, ssk, k1, turn = 6 sts.

- **Shape instep:** Using the same heel flap needle, pick up 4 sts along left edge of heel flap. Work across top of foot, transferring these 10 sts onto one needle. With a third needle, pick up 4 sts along second heel flap edge and k first 3 sts of heel. Place marker here for beg of next rnd.
- Work in rnds, adjusting so that there are 8 sts on each needle (24 sts total). Work 1 rnd even. On next rnd, decrease as follows: at end of needle 1, ssk. Repeat these 2 rnds until there are 16 sts. Work 2 rnds even or until foot measures ½" less than desired length.
- **Shape toe:** K 1 rnd even. Decrease on next rnd as follows: At end of needle 1, k last 2 sts tog. At beg of needle 2, ssk. At end of needle 2, k2tog. At beg of needle 3, ssk. Work 1 rnd even. Repeat these two rnds, dec 4 sts every other rnd, until there are 8 sts. Break yarn, leaving a 5" tail. Place sts of needles 1 and 3 on one needle. There should now be 4 sts each on two needles. Refer to Kitchener Stitch on page 122. Weave toe, using Kitchener st.

Wee Dot Sock Graph & Wee Striped Sock Graph

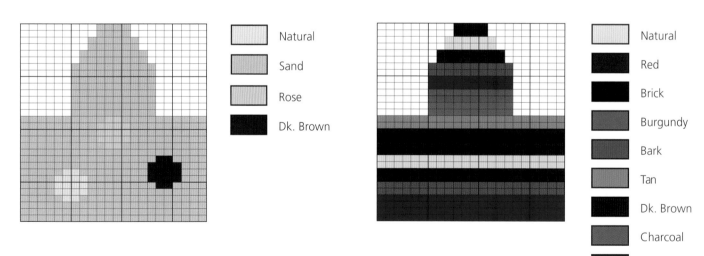

Natural
Sand
Rose
Dk. Brown

Natural
Red
Brick
Burgundy
Bark
Tan
Dk. Brown
Charcoal
Black

WEE DOT JUMPER

Front and Back

(make two)

- Using spn and color of choice, CO 28 sts.
- Work in K1P1 ribbing for 3 rows.
- Work in st st for 3 rows, following the Wee Dot Jumper Graph.
- On next row, make first decrease on both sides. Continue decreasing on every fifth row until there are 20 sts.
- Continue, following the graph until complete and piece is 3" from the bottom.
- Change color and work in K1P1 ribbing for 10 rows, decreasing 1 st on each side on Row 6 and Row 9.
- On Row 11, work 4 sts for each shoulder strap and BO the center 8 sts. Work each shoulder strap in ribbing for 11 rows. Put 4 sts on a holder.
- K shoulder tog from front to back.
- Sew front and back pieces tog, leaving a 1¾" opening for the armhole.
- Using crochet hook, SC 1 row around armholes and around neck in a CC.

Bottom Scallop

- Using crochet hook, SC 1, skip 2 sts; in the next st, crochet ★3 DC, skip 2 sts.★ Repeat from ★ to ★ around bottom of skirt.

	Creme		Raspberry
	Sand		Mahogany
	Rose		

Have a ball!

When shopping for yarn, don't be afraid to purchase the end of a dye lot or just a few remaining balls of a color or texture. You can always find a way to use small amounts of yarn when knitting intarsia.

WEE STRIPED SCARF

(not shown in photograph)

Scarf

- Using spn and color of choice, CO 7 sts.
- Work in st st for 8" changing colors every 2 rows.
- BO.

Finishing

- Add 1" fringe onto both ends, using all the colors.

WEE STRIPED CARDIGAN

Back

- Using spn and color of choice, CO 20 sts.
- Work in K1P1 ribbing for 3 rows.
- Work in st st, changing colors every 2 rows and following the Wee Striped Cardigan Graph until piece measures 4" from beg.
- Put 7 sts on holder for right shoulder, 13 sts on holder for back of neck, and 7 sts on holder for left shoulder.

Left Front

- Using spn and color of choice, CO 15 sts.
- Work in K1P1 ribbing for 3 rows.
- Work in st st, changing colors every 2 rows and following the graph until piece measures 3" from beg, ending on a purl row.
- **Shape neck:** On neck edge, put 5 sts on a holder. Decrease every other row at neck edge until 7 sts rem, put on holder.

Right Front

- Work same as for left front, reversing shaping for shoulder and neck.
- K shoulders tog from the inside.

Sleeve

- For sleeve, pick up 26 sts, 13 on either side of the shoulder; picking up 3 and skipping 1, all along.
- Work in st st, following the Wee Striped Cardigan Sleeve Graph on page 77, changing colors every 2 rows.
- Decrease on every fifth row on both sides of the sleeve three times until there are 20 sts. Always decrease 1 st from the edge. On the right side of the sleeve, decrease by skp; on the left side decrease by k2tog.
- Work in K1P1 ribbing for 4 rows.
- BO loosely.
- Sew sweater tog, matching underarm seams.

Neck

- Pick up 38 sts around the neck.
- Work in K1P1 ribbing for 4 rows.
- BO.

Left Placket

- Pick up 25 sts.
- Work in K1P1 ribbing for 3 rows.
- BO.

Right Placket

- Pick up 25 sts.
- Make buttonholes on the first row. Work in K1P1 ribbing for 3 sts, BO 1 st, work 8 sts, BO 1 st, work 8 sts, BO 1 st, work 4 sts.
- On next row, CO 1 st where you BO. Continue in K1P1 ribbing for a total of 3 rows.
- BO.
- Sew on three buttons.

Wee Striped Cardigan Graph

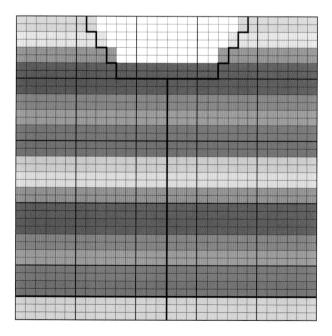

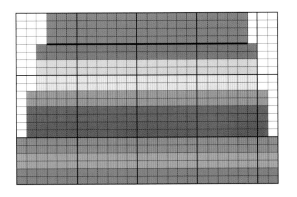

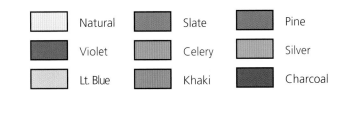

Natural	Slate	Pine
Violet	Celery	Silver
Lt. Blue	Khaki	Charcoal

WEE DOT HAT

Wee Dot Hat Graph

Hat

- Using spn and color of choice, CO 41 sts.
- Change to CC and work in st st for 6 rows.
- K 10 rows in pattern, following Wee Dot Hat Graph.
- Beg decreasing for top:
  - Row 1: ★K2tog, k6★ (5 times), k1
  - Row 2: P
  - Row 3: ★K2tog, k5★ (5 times), k1
  - Row 4: P
  - Row 5: ★K2tog, k4★ (5 times), k1
  - Row 6: P4, p2tog, ★p3, p2tog★ (4 times)
  - Row 7: ★K2tog, k2★ (5 times), k1
  - Row 8: P2, p2tog, ★p1, p2tog★ (4 times)
  - Row 9: K2tog all around until there are 7 sts.
- K 20 rows.
- Sew tog.
- Knot at top if desired.

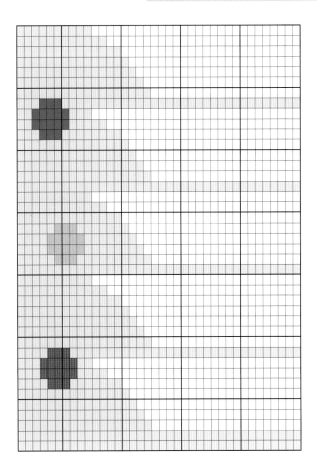

Natural	Raspberry	
Sand	Burgundy	

Jesse's Topknot Hat and Cardigan

JESSE'S TOPKNOT HAT

Materials

YARN

100% wool, handspun, sportweight

CC (A) - Black
CC (B) - Blue Gray
CC (C) - Charcoal
CC (D) - Dk Green
CC (E) - Gold
CC (F) - Indigo
CC (G) - Natural
CC (H) - Olive
CC (I) - Pine
CC (J) - Royal
CC (K) - Slate

NOTIONS

Single-pointed knitting needles, size 4, or size to obtain gauge

Yarn needle

MEASUREMENT

approximately 20" around

GAUGE

6 sts x 8 rows = 1"

STITCH PATTERNS

St st, K1P1 ribbing

Hat

- Using spn and color C, CO on 122 sts.
- Work in K1P1 ribbing for 8 rows, following Jesse's Topknot Hat Graph on pages 80–81.
- Work in st st for 30 rows in pattern, changing color every 2 rows.
- Beg decreasing on the next row:

  Row 1: K1, ★k2tog, k18★ (6 times), k1
  Row 2 (and all even rows until Row 34): P
  Row 3: K1, ★k2tog, k17★ (6 times), k1
  Row 5: K1, ★k2tog, k16★ (6 times), k1
  Row 7: K1, ★k2tog, k15★ (6 times), k1
  Row 9: K1, ★k2tog, k14★ (6 times), k1
  Row 11: K1, ★k2tog, k13★ (6 times), k1
  Row 13: K1, ★k2tog, k12★ (6 times), k1
  Row 15: K1, ★k2tog, k11★ (6 times), k1
  Row 17: K1, ★k2tog, k10★ (6 times), k1
  Row 19: K1, ★k2tog, k9★ (6 times), k1
  Row 21: K1, ★k2tog, k8★ (6 times), k1
  Row 23: K1, ★k2tog, k7★ (6 times), k1
  Row 25: K1, ★k2tog, k6★ (6 times), k1
  Row 27: K1, ★k2tog, k5★ (6 times), k1
  Row 29: K1, ★k2tog, k4★ (6 times), k1
  Row 31: K1, ★k2tog, k3★ (6 times), k1
  Row 33: K1, ★k2tog, k2★ (6 times), k1 = 20 sts
  Rows 34–38: K
  Row 39: K1, ★k2tog, k1★ (6 times), k1 = 14 sts
  Rows 40–44: K
  Row 45: K1, ★k2tog★ (6 times), k1 = 8 sts.

- K these 8 sts for 39 rows, or to desired length, changing colors every 2 rows, following the graph.
- Using yarn needle, draw these sts tog and tie off inside hat.

Finishing

- Seam back of hat, making certain to seam first 8 rows on brim approximately 1" on the reverse side. This is so that when the brim is turned up, the seam does not show.

Natural

Gold

Blue Gray

Slate

Royal

Indigo

Olive

Pine

Dk. Green

Charcoal

Black

Color-photocopy the graph sections. Piece the photocopies together with Section 1 at the left, and Section 2 at the right. Begin knitting at the bottom-right corner of the graph and work to the left and up.

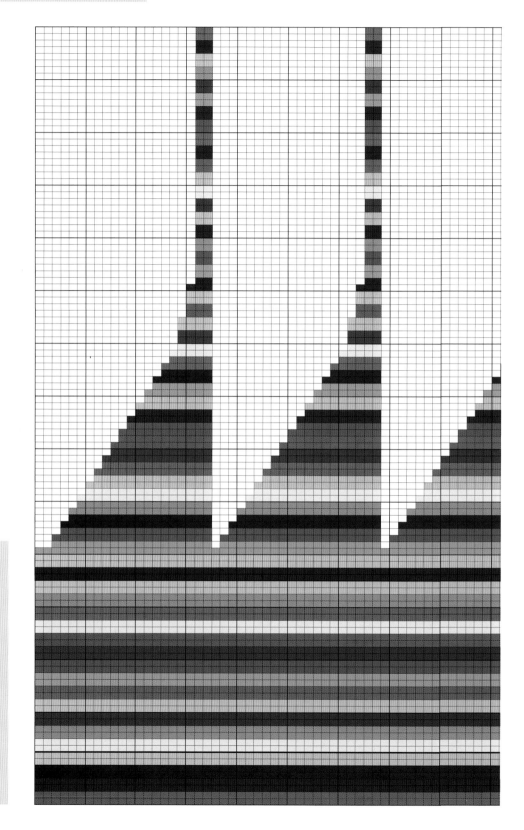

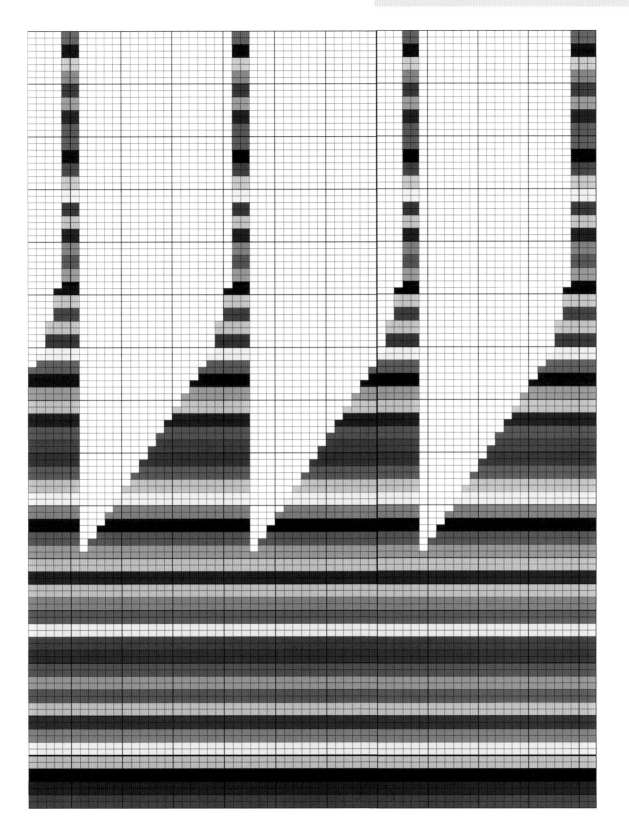

JESSE'S CARDIGAN

Materials

YARN

100% wool, handspun, sportweight

CC (A) - Black

CC (B) - Blue Gray

CC (C) - Charcoal

CC (D) - Dk Green

CC (E) - Gold

CC (F) - Indigo

CC (G) - Natural

CC (H) - Olive

CC (I) - Pine

CC (J) - Royal

CC (K) - Slate

NOTIONS

Buttons, 5 (6, 7)

Single-pointed knitting needles, size 4, or size to obtain gauge

MEASUREMENTS

Size: 4 (6, 8) years

Length: 16" (20", 22")

Chest: 13" (15", 19")

Sleeve: 12" (17", 20½")

GAUGE

6 sts x 8 rows = 1"

STITCH PATTERNS

St st, K1P1 ribbing

Back

- Using spn and color K, CO 76 (90, 112) sts.
- Work in K1P1 ribbing for 10 rows, changing colors every 2 rows, following Jesse's Cardigan Graph on pages 84–86.
- Change to st st and continue following the graph.
- **Shape armhole:** Beg at row 73 (98, 109).
- Small: BO 2 sts at the beg of the next 2 rows (one time each side). Decrease 1 st on each side of body on every other row one time and on every fourth row two times.
- Medium: BO 3 sts at the beg of the next 2 rows (one time each side). Decrease 1 st on each side of the body every other row 1 time, and on every third row two times.
- Large: BO 3 sts at the beg of the next 2 rows (one time each side). Decrease every row one time on every fourth row three times.
- For all sizes, continue following the graph.
- **Shape neck:** Beg at row 125 (159, 163).
- Put center 36 sts on a holder for the back of the neck.
- Work each side separately, decreasing at neck edge every other row two times (two times, three times) until 15 sts (20, 25) remain. Put these sts on holder.

Left and Right Fronts

(make two, reversing shaping)

- Using spn and color K, CO 38 sts (45, 56).
- Work in K1P1 ribbing for 10 rows, changing colors every 2 rows, following the graph.
- Change to st st and continue following the graph.
- **Shape armhole**: Beg at row 73 (98, 109). Work as for back, shaping armhole only at edge opposite armhole.
- For all sizes, continue following the graph.
- **Shape neck:** Beg at row 125 (159, 163).
- At neck edge, put 8 sts on a holder and decrease every other row at neck edge 12 times (12 times, 13 times), always decreasing 1 st in from the edge until 14 (19, 24) sts rem.
- Put these sts on a holder.

Sleeves

- Using spn and color K, CO 43 (47, 51) sts.
- Work in K1P1 ribbing for 8 rows, following Jesse's Cardigan Sleeve Graph on pages 87–89.
- Work in st st for 5 (8, 3) rows, following the graph, then increase 1 st each side. Continue in pattern, increasing 1 st each side on every fifth row until you have 71 (97, 103) sts.
- K 5 rows.
- For all sizes: Decrease 1 st at each end every row four times. BO 2 sts each end two times (two times, three times). BO 4 sts each end one time (four times, five times). BO rem sts.

Finishing

- K shoulders together.
- Seam body.
- Seam sleeve.
- Sew sleeve onto body.

Neck Ribbing Finishing

- Pick up 75 sts (75, 81) around the neck.
- Work in K1P1 ribbing for 10 rows, starting with a p st on the right side and ending with a p st on the left side, and changing colors every 2 rows.
- BO loosely.

Placket Finishing

- Pick up 84 sts (102, 120) for each side of the placket by picking up 3 sts, skip 1 all the way along the side, 1 st in from the edge.
- Work in K1P1 ribbing for 6 rows, changing colors every 2 rows.
- For button side, make buttonholes on the third row.
- Space five (six, seven) buttonholes evenly along placket making certain one button is 2 sts from the top and one is 2 sts from the bottom.
- On the third row, BO 2 sts for each buttonhole. CO those 2 sts on the fourth row. This will create the buttonhole.
- Sew on buttons.

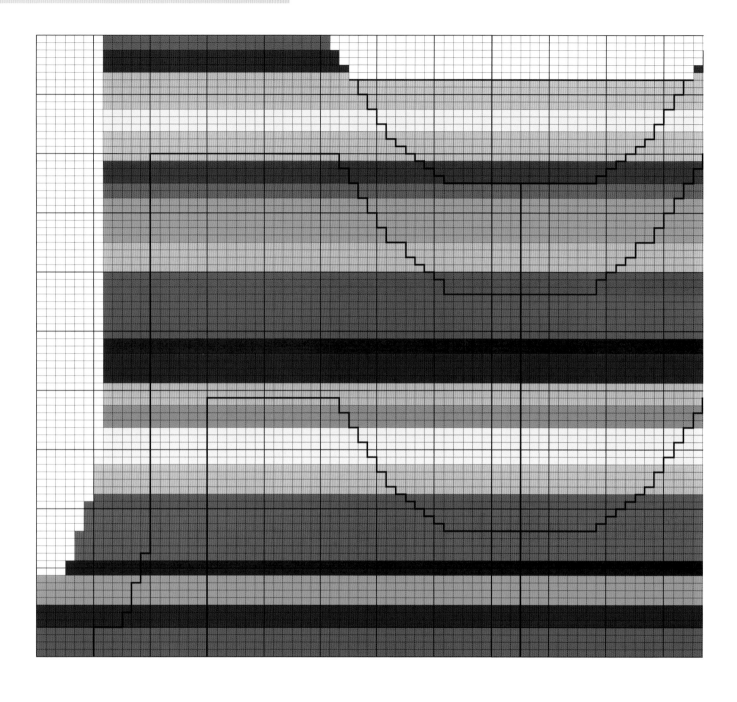

Natural	Blue Gray	Royal	Olive
Gold	Slate	Indigo	Pine

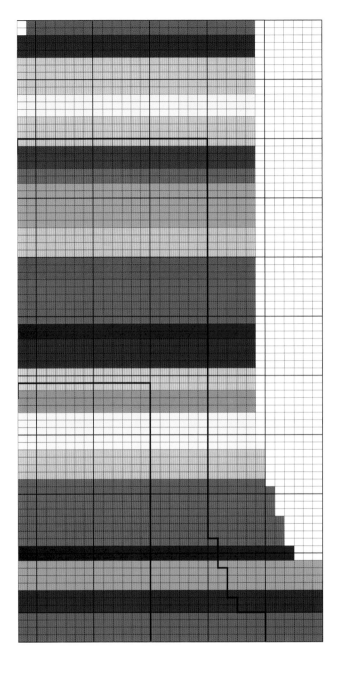

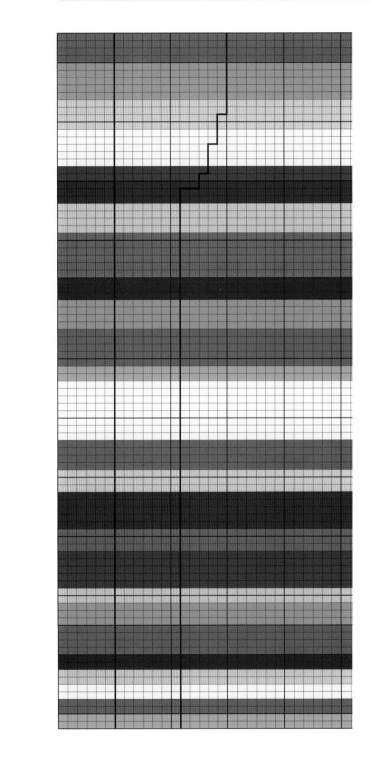

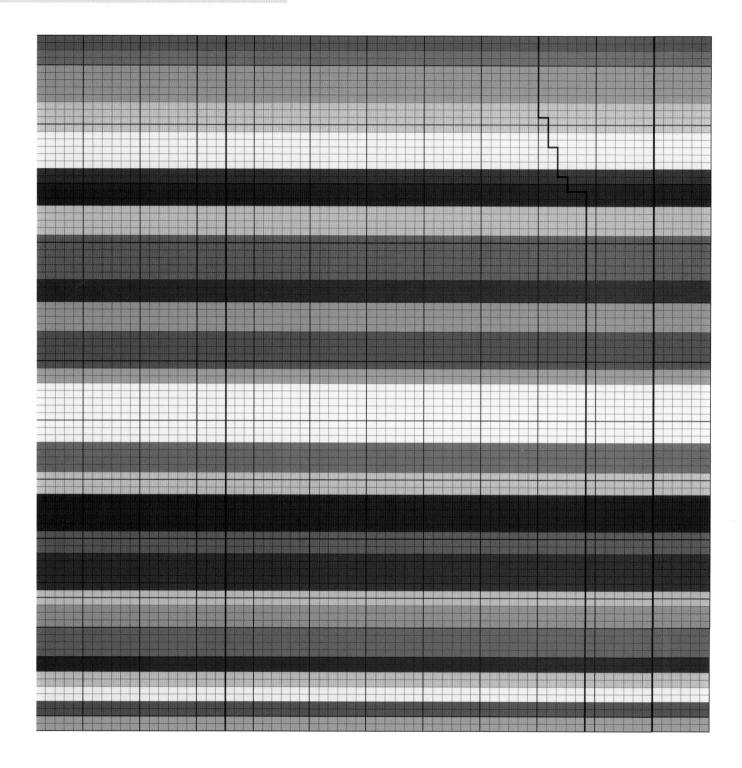

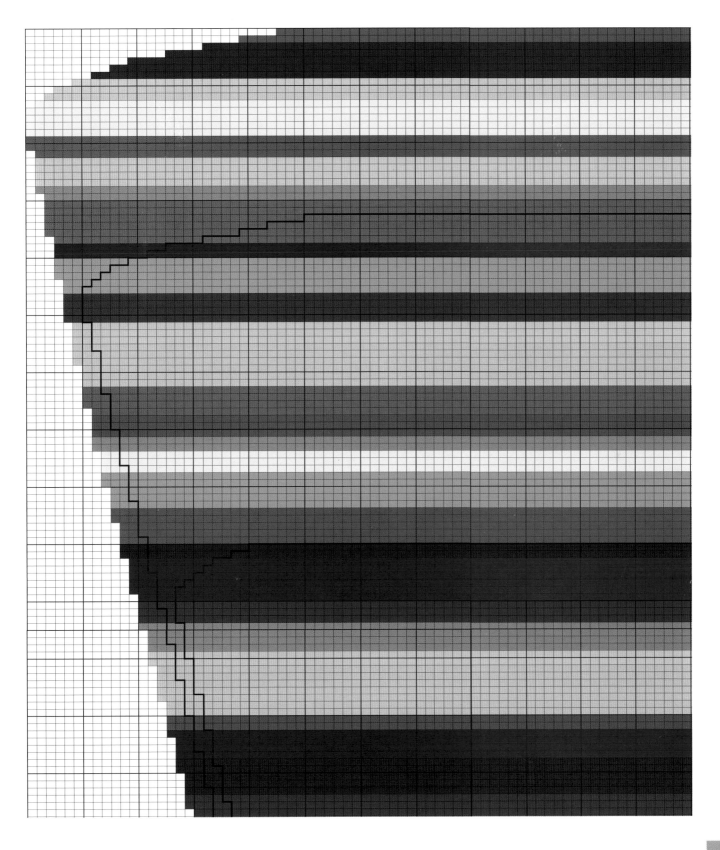

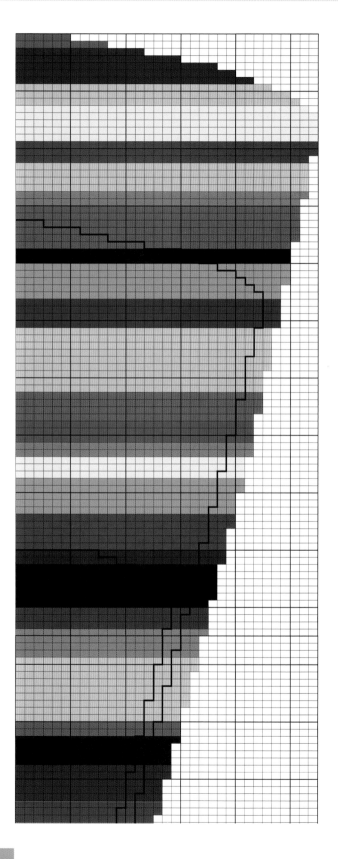

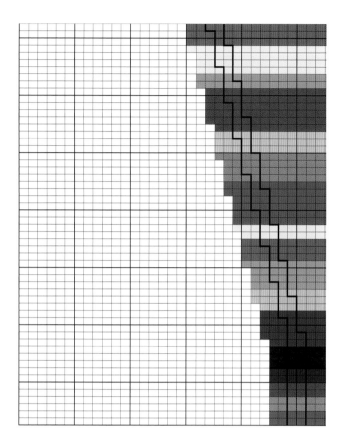

For both the Jesse's Cardigan Graph and the Jesse's Cardigan Sleeve Graph, color-photocopy the graph sections. Piece the photocopies together with Section 1 at the top left, Section 2 at the top right, Section 3 at the bottom left, and Section 4 at the bottom right. (See Jesse's Cardigan Map and Jesse's Cardigan Sleeve Map on page 89.) Begin knitting at the bottom-right corner of the graph and work to the left and up.

...

A stitch in time
Once you have completed construction of a garment, weave a length of yarn through each side seam. If, at some point, you should need to fix a hole in the garment, you will have mending yarn at hand that matches perfectly.

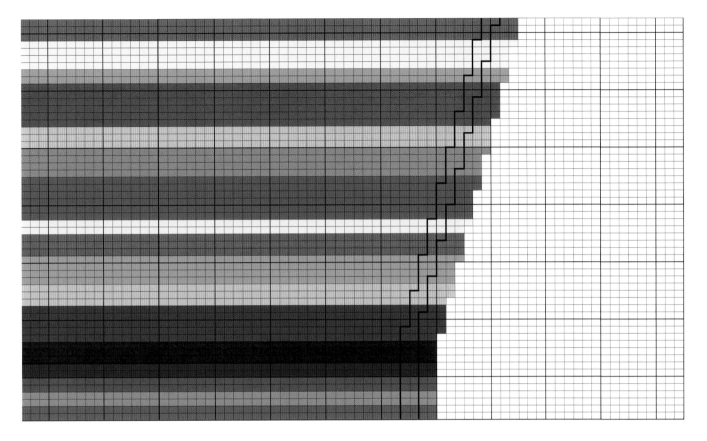

Jesse's Cardigan Map

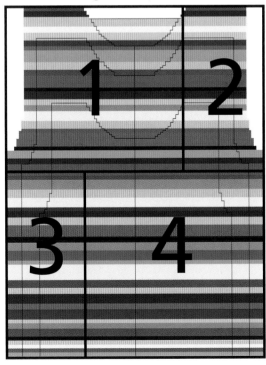

Jesse's Cardigan Sleeve Map

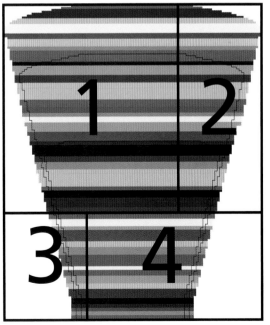

Striped Mitten and Companion Topknot Hat

STRIPED MITTEN

Materials

YARN

100% wool, handspun, sportweight
Contrasting colors (11)

NOTIONS

Double-pointed knitting
needles, size 4

Single-pointed knitting needles,
size 4, or size to obtain gauge

Yarn needle

MEASUREMENT

fits woman's hand

GAUGE

6 sts x 8 rows = 1"

STITCH PATTERNS

St st, K1P1 ribbing

Body of Mitten

- Using spn and color of choice, CO 50 sts.
- Work in K1P1 ribbing for 40 rows, changing colors every other row.
- On next row, change to st st and increase 6 sts evenly spaced across this first row.
- Work in stripe pattern for 6 rows.

Thumb Gusset

- Continue in st st and striping pattern, increasing on every other row at the beg and the end of the row until there are 66 sts. Always increase 1 st in from the edge.
- K for 5 rows in pattern.
- Break yarn.

Thumb Opening

- Put the first 8 sts on a holder.
- Join yarn and k in striping pattern until 8 sts rem.
- Put these 8 sts on a holder. These 16 sts are for the thumb.
- Work in striping pattern for 30 rows, ending with a purl row.

Top of Mitten

- Continue in pattern and beg decrease, or shaping, for the top of the mitten.

  Row 1: K1, skp, k20, k2tog, skp, k20, k2tog, k1
  Row 2 (and all even rows until Row 12): P
  Row 3: K1, skp, k18, k2tog, skp, k18, k2tog, k1
  Row 5: K1, skp, k16, k2tog, skp, k16, k2tog, k1
  Row 7: K1, skp, k14, k2tog, skp, k14, k2tog, k1
  Row 9: K1, skp, k12, k2tog, skp, k12, k2tog, k1
  Row 11: K1, skp, k10, k2tog, skp, k10, k2tog, k1
  Row 12: P1, p2tog, p8, p2tog, p2tog, p8, p2tog, p1
  Row 13: K1, skp, k6, k2tog, skp, k6, k2tog, k1

Row 14: P1, p2tog, p4, p2tog, p2tog, p4, p2tog, p1

Row 15: K1, skp, k2, k2tog, skp, k2, k2tog, k1 until there are 10 sts.

- Refer to Kitchener Stitch on page 122. At this point, fold mitten in half and use the Kitchener st to connect 5 sts to 5 sts on either side of mitten.
- Seam mitten tog, leaving the hole for the thumb open.

Thumb

- Using dpn and MC, divide 16 sts on holder evenly on three needles, making certain not to twist sts in the round.
- Mark beg.
- K for 12 rows, matching the striping pattern from the body of the mitten.
- Beg decrease, or shaping, for thumb:

Row 1: K2tog, k2tog, k8, k2tog, k2tog

Row 2: K

Row 3: K2tog, k2tog, k4, k2tog, k2tog

Row 4: K2tog all the way around until there are 4 sts.

- Using yarn needle, draw these sts tog and bury in the weave.

COMPANION TOPKNOT HAT

Materials

YARN
100% wool, handspun, sportweight
Contrasting colors (11)

NOTIONS
Single-pointed knitting needles, size 4, or size to obtain gauge
Yarn needle

MEASUREMENT
Approximately 22" around

GAUGE
6 sts x 8 rows = 1"

STITCH PATTERNS
St st, K1P1 ribbing

Hat

- Using spn and color of choice, CO on 142 sts.
- Work in K1P1 ribbing for 8 rows.
- Work in st st for 40 rows, changing color every 2 rows.
- On the next row, beg decreases:

  Row 1: K1, ★k2tog, k18★ (7 times), k1
  Row 2 (and all even rows until Row 34): P
  Row 3: K1, ★k2tog, k17★ (7 times), k1
  Row 5: K1, ★k2tog, k16★ (7 times), k1
  Row 7: K1, ★k2tog, k15★ (7 times), k1
  Row 9: K1, ★k2tog, k14★ (7 times), k1
  Row 11: K1, ★k2tog, k13★ (7 times), k1
  Row 13: K1, ★k2tog, k12★ (7 times), k1
  Row 15: K1, ★k2tog, k11★ (7 times), k1
  Row 17: K1, ★k2tog, k10★ (7 times), k1
  Row 19: K1, ★k2tog, k9★ (7 times), k1
  Row 21: K1, ★k2tog, k8★ (7 times), k1
  Row 23: K1, ★k2tog, k7★ (7 times), k1
  Row 25: K1, ★k2tog, k6★ (7 times), k1
  Row 27: K1, ★k2tog, k5★ (7 times), k1
  Row 29: K1, ★k2tog, k4★ (7 times), k1
  Row 31: K1, ★k2tog, k3★ (7 times), k1
  Row 33: K1, ★k2tog, k2★ (7 times), k1 = 28 sts
  Rows 34–38: K
  Row 39: K1, ★k2tog, k1★ (7 times), k1 = 16 sts.

- Work these 16 sts for 39 rows, changing colors every 2 rows.
- Using yarn needle, draw these sts tog and tie off inside hat.

Finishing

- Seam back of hat, making certain to seam first 8 rows on brim approximately 1" on the reverse side. This is so that when the brim is turned up, the seam does not show.

Leftovers:
Never throw away your scraps. A pile of little ends and random scraps can be used to make a variegated ball of yarn. They can also be just right for making into doll clothes.

Ruby's Daisy Hat and Sweater

Ruby's Daisy Hat and Sweater

RUBY'S DAISY HAT

Materials

YARN

100% wool, handspun, sportweight

MC - Celery
CC (A) - Butter
CC (B) - Orange
CC (C) - Pine
CC (D) - Pink
CC (E) - Rust
CC (F) - Slate
CC (G) - Violet

NOTIONS

Single-pointed knitting needles, size 4, or size to obtain gauge

Yarn needle

MEASUREMENT

approximately 20" around

GAUGE

6 sts x 8 rows = 1"

STITCH PATTERN

St st

Hat

- Using spn and MC, CO 122 sts.
- Change to color B and work in st st for 8 rows.
- Change to MC and work until piece measures 4" (unrolled), following Ruby's Daisy Hat Graph on page 95.
- On a knit row, beg decreases, following the graph.
    Row 1: K1, ★k2tog, k18★ (6 times), k1
    Row 2 (and all even rows until Row 20): P
    Row 3: K1, ★k2tog, k17★ (6 times), k1
    Row 5: K1, ★k2tog, k16★ (6 times), k1
    Row 7: K1, ★k2tog, k15★ (6 times), k1
    Row 9: K1, ★k2tog, k14★ (6 times), k1
    Row 11: K1, ★k2tog, k13★ (6 times), k1
    Row 13: K1, ★k2tog, k12★ (6 times), k1
    Row 15: K1, ★k2tog, k11★ (6 times), k1
    Row 17: K1, ★k2tog, k10★ (6 times), k1
    Row 19: K1, ★k2tog, k9★ (6 times), k1
    Row 20: P1, ★p8, p2tog★ (6 times), p1
    Row 21: K1, ★k2tog, k7★ (6 times), k1
    Row 22: P1, ★p6, p2tog★ (6 times), p1
    Row 23: K1, ★k2tog, k5★ (6 times), k1
    Row 24: P1, ★p4, p2tog★ (6 times), p1
    Row 25: K1, ★k2tog, k3★ (6 times), k1
    Row 26: P1, ★p2, p2tog★ (6 times), p1
    Row 27: K1, ★k2tog, k1★ (6 times), k1
    Row 28: P1, ★p2tog all around★ (6 times), p1 until there are 8 sts.
- Using yarn needle, draw these sts tog and tie off inside hat.

Finishing

- Seam back of hat, making certain to seam brim on the reverse side. This is so that when the brim is turned up the seam does not show.

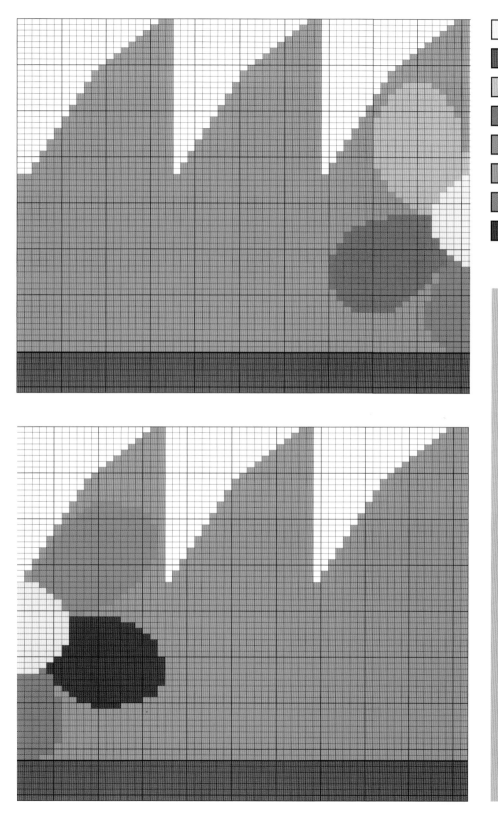

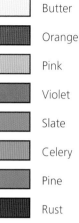

	Butter
	Orange
	Pink
	Violet
	Slate
	Celery
	Pine
	Rust

Color-photocopy the graph sections. Piece the photocopies together with Section 1 at the top, and Section 2 at the bottom, joining the flower design. Begin knitting at the bottom-right corner of the graph and work to the left and up.

Unwanted ridges
Always try to finish a row before putting your work down, especially if you know you won't be getting back to it for several days. Leaving your needles in the work can set the yarn, causing a ridge that can be quite difficult to remove from the fabric.

RUBY'S DAISY SWEATER

Materials

YARN

100% wool, handspun, sportweight

    MC - Gold

    CC (A) - Orange

    CC (B) - Slate

    CC (C) - Celery

    CC (D) - Violet

NOTIONS

Double-pointed knitting needles, size 4, or size to obtain gauge

Single-pointed knitting needles, size 4, or size to obtain gauge

MEASUREMENTS

Size: 4 (6, 8) years

Length: 16" (20", 22")

Chest: 13" (15", 19")

Sleeve: 12" (17", 20½")

GAUGE

6 sts x 8 rows = 1"

STITCH PATTERN

St st

Sweater Back

- Using spn and color A, CO 76 (90, 102) sts.
- Work in st st for 10 rows.
- Change to MC and continue, following Ruby's Daisy Sweater Graph on pages 98–100.
- **Shape armhole:** Beg at row 81 (105, 117).
- Small: BO 2 sts at the beg of the next 2 rows (one time each side). Decrease 1 st on each side of body on every other row one time and on every fourth row two times.

- Medium: BO 3 sts at the beg of the next 2 rows (one time each side). Decrease 1 st on each side of the body every other row one time, and on every fourth row two times.
- Large: BO 3 sts at the beg of the next 2 rows (one time each side). Decrease every other row one time, and on every fourth row three times.
- For all sizes, continue following the graph.
- **Shape neck:** Divide sts for shoulders and back of neck.
- Put center 36 (40, 42) sts on a holder for the back of the neck.
- Put 14 (19, 23) sts on a separate holder for each shoulder.

Sweater Front

- Knit same as for back until row 118 (147, 171).
- **Shape neck:** Put center 16 sts on a holder and dec every row five times (six times, seven times), and every other row six times (seven times, seven times), always decreasing 1 st in from the edge until 14 (19, 23) sts rem on each shoulder.
- Put these sts on a separate holder.

Sleeves

- Using spn and color B, CO 44 (48, 52) sts.
- Work in st st for 8 rows following Ruby's Daisy Sweater Sleeve Graph on pages 101–103.
- Change to MC.
- K 3 (5, 2) rows then increase 1 st each side. Continue increasing 1 st each side on every fifth row until there are 73 (93, 105) sts.
- K 5 rows.
- Dec 1 st at each end every row four times (three times, three times). BO 2 sts each end two times (two times, three times). BO four sts each end one time (four times, four times). BO rem sts.

Finishing

- Knit shoulders tog from the inside.
- Seam front and back tog up to the armholes, making certain to reverse sewing for the bottom 10 rows where the ribbing rolls.
- Sew sleeve tog up to top shaping.
- Sew sleeve onto body.

Neck

- Using dpn and color C, pick up all sts around the neck.
- Work in st st for 10 rows and BO loosely.

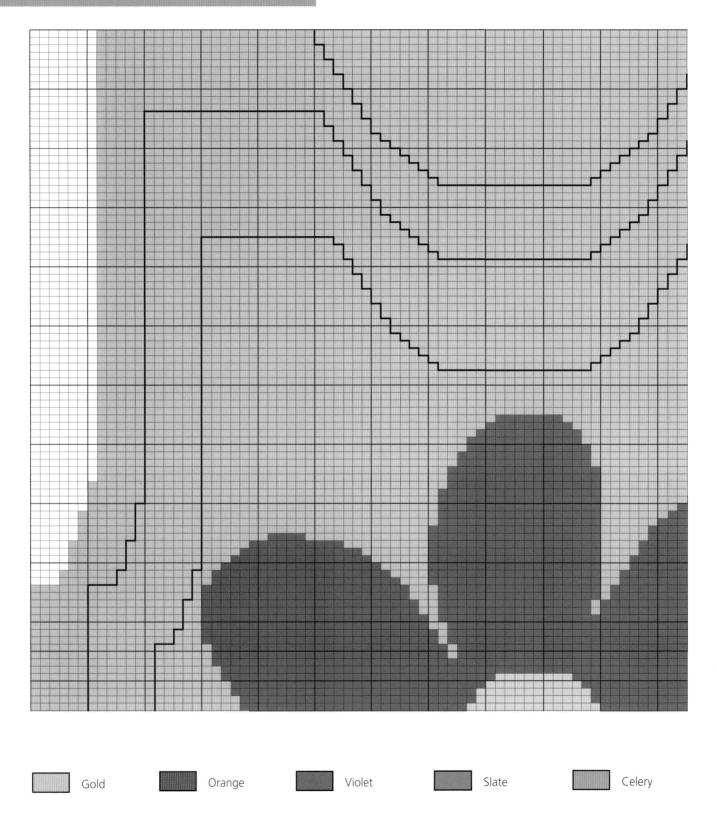

Gold   Orange   Violet   Slate   Celery

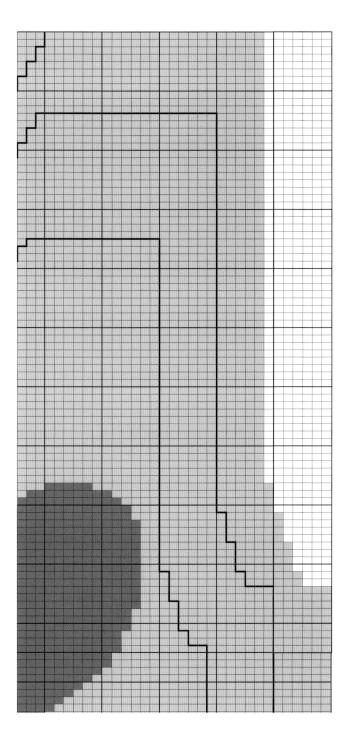

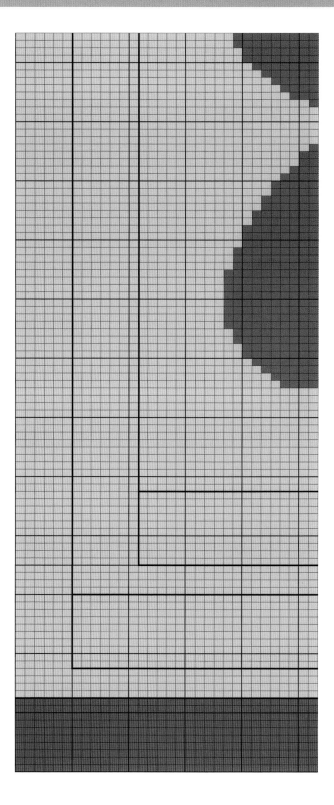

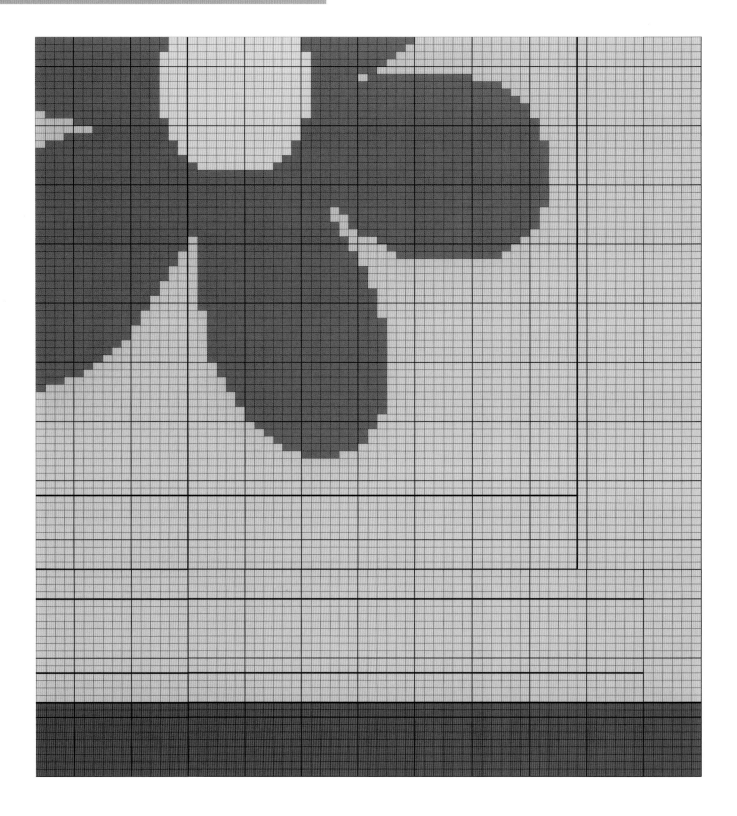

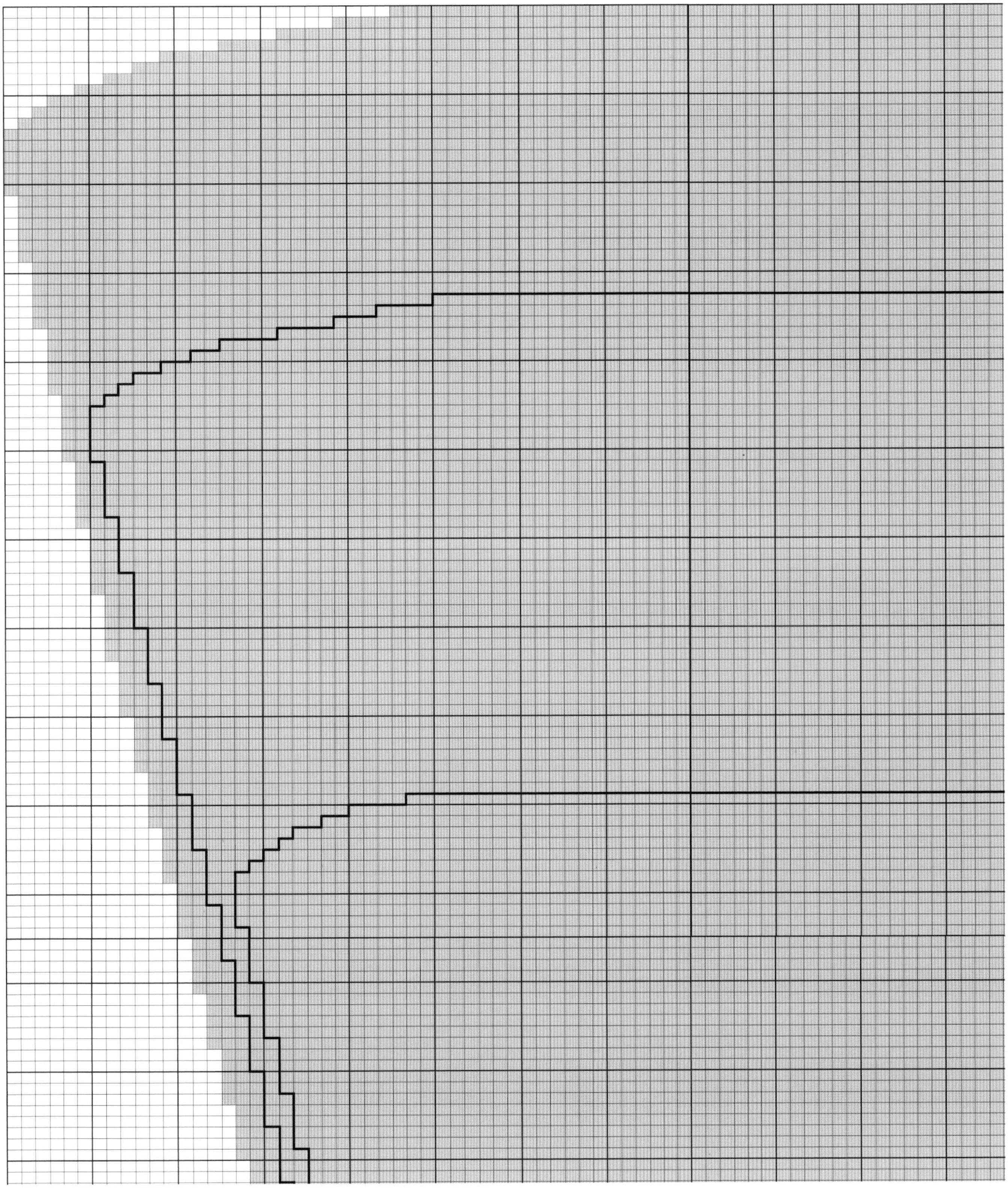

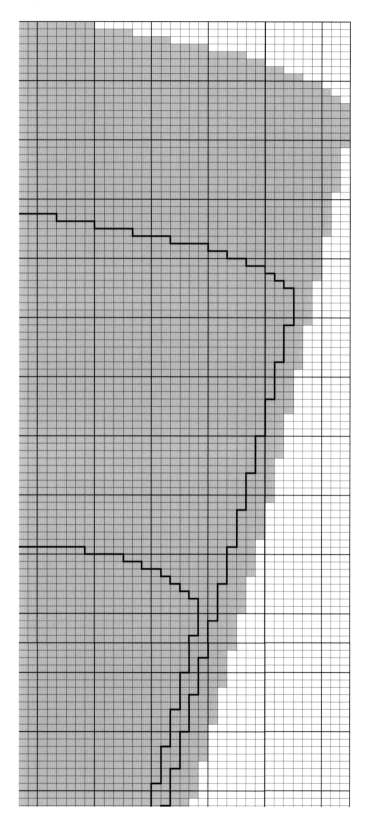

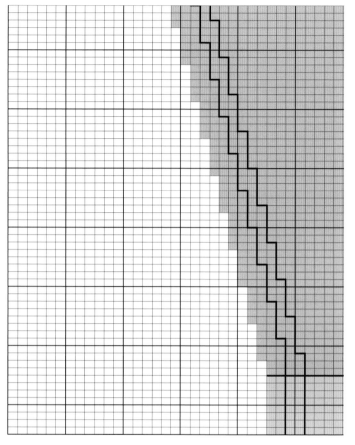

For both the Ruby's Daisy Sweater Graph and the Ruby's Daisy Sweater Sleeve Graph, color-photocopy the graph sections. Piece the photocopies together with Section 1 at the top left, Section 2 at the top right, Section 3 at the bottom left, and Section 4 at the bottom right. (See Ruby's Daisy Sweater Map and Ruby's Daisy Sweater Sleeve Map on page 103.) Begin knitting at the bottom-right corner of the graph and work to the left and up.

...

Join in the fun
Always try to join a new ball of yarn at the beginning of a row. You will be able to gauge whether you have enough yarn to complete the row by spreading out your work and checking to see if the remaining yarn will cover the width four times.

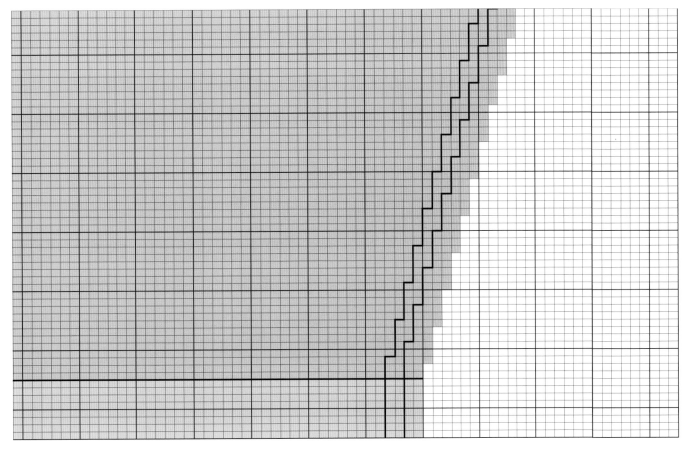

Ruby's Daisy Sweater Map

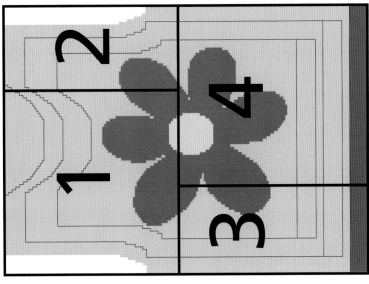

Ruby's Daisy Sweater Sleeve Map

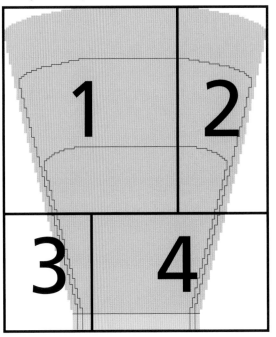

Ruby's Bunny

Materials

YARN

100% wool, handspun, sportweight

Any number of colors
(see graphs)

NOTIONS

Single-pointed knitting needles,
size 4, or size to obtain gauge

Yarn needle

MEASUREMENT

small, fits a 16" doll

GAUGE

6 sts x 8 rows = 1"

STITCH PATTERNS

St st, K1P1 ribbing

RUBY'S BUNNY DAISY SWEATER

Sweater Back

- Using spn and CC, CO 36 sts.
- Work in st st for 4 rows.
- Change to MC and work, following the Ruby's Bunny Daisy Sweater Graph on page 105 for 43 rows.
- **Shape back of neck:** K10 sts, k2tog, k to within 11 sts of end, skp, and k10 sts. Put center 12 sts on a holder for back of neck.
- K 2 rows on left shoulder, then put these sts on a holder.
- On right side, change color and work in K1P1 ribbing for 4 rows for inside neck placket.
- BO.

Sweater Front

- Using spn and CC, CO 36 sts.
- Work in st st for 4 rows.
- Change to MC and work for 31 rows (including first 4 rows), following the graph.
- **Shape neck:** Put center 8 sts on a holder and work each side separately. Decrease on every other row four times at neck edge on each side. Remember to decrease 1 st in from the edge. For left slant, use skp; for

right slant, use k2tog. Use appropriate decrease for each side of the neck.

- Four rows before the top on the left side, change color and work in K1P1 ribbing, continuing to decrease at neck edge. After 2 rows, make a small buttonhole by BO 1 st halfway across the row and CO this st again, on the next row.
- BO this side and put the other side on holder.

Shoulders

- Match shoulder tog. K shoulder tog from inside.
- On left side, there will be a small placket with one buttonhole in front and a small placket to sew one button onto on the back. Sew small button on. This will allow a doll or animal with a large head to fit through sweater neck opening.

Sleeve

Note: On the left side (where your small placket is), overlap both plackets, just as they are when buttoned before picking up sts. The needle will go through both layers as if they were one when picking up this side.

- Pick up 30 sts, with 15 on either side of the shoulder—pick up 3 sts, skip 1 st, all along.
- Using MC, work in st st, decreasing on every eighth row three times until there are 24 sts.
- Work in st st for 6 more rows.
- Change to CC and work 4 more rows.
- BO loosely.
- Repeat for other sleeve.
- Sew sweater tog, matching underarm seams.

Neck

- Pick up 56 sts around the neck, starting at the shoulder placket and work back and forth for 4 rows.
- BO, leaving an opening where shoulder placket is.

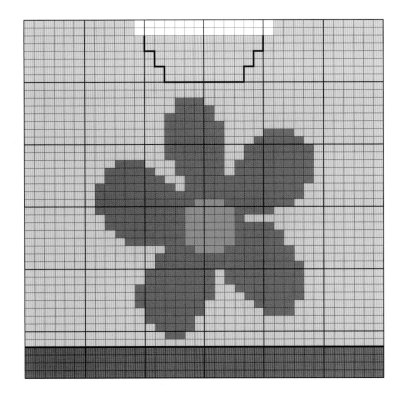

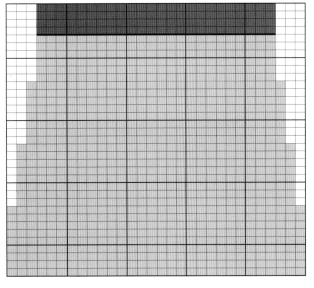

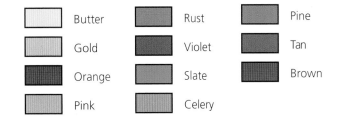

	Butter		Rust		Pine
	Gold		Violet		Tan
	Orange		Slate		Brown
	Pink		Celery		

RUBY'S BUNNY DOT SKIRT

Front and Back

(make two)

- Using spn and color of choice, CO 40 sts.
- Work in K1P1 ribbing for 4 rows.
- Work in st st, following Ruby's Bunny Dot Skirt Graph and decreasing on every fifth row until there are 28 sts.
- Work in K1P1 ribbing for 5 rows.
- BO.
- Sew front and back tog.
- Make a twisted string 20" long.
- Thread through skirt, over 3 sts and under 3 sts, starting at center front.

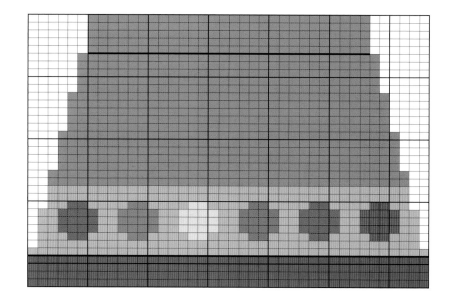

Ruby's Bunny Dot Skirt Graph

RUBY'S BUNNY SOCK

Sock

- Using spn and color of choice, CO 22 sts loosely.
- Work in st st, following Ruby's Bunny Sock Graph, until sock measures 1¾".
- Change to dpn, dividing sts evenly on three needles, and connect sts taking care not to twist them.
- K 2 rnds before beg shaping.
- **Divide for heel:** Place 5 sts on each of two needles for top of foot, and 10 sts on the rem needle for the heel flap. If the small size of the sock makes working the heel difficult, place the foot sts on a holder or string to keep them out of the way.
- **Heel flap:** Work in st st for ½", ending with a right side row.
- **Turn heel:**

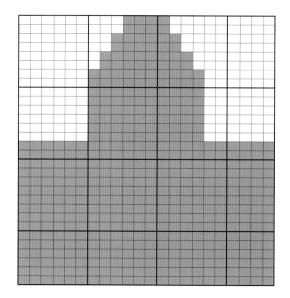

Ruby's Bunny Sock Graph

Row 1: P to center of heel flap, p next 2 sts tog, p1, turn
Row 2: Sl 1, k1, ssk, k1, turn
Row 3: Sl 1, p2, p2tog, p1, turn
Row 4: Sl 1, k3, ssk, k1, turn = 6 sts.

- **Shape instep:** Using the same heel flap needle, pick up 4 sts along left edge of heel flap. Work across top of foot, transferring these 10 sts onto one needle. With a third needle, pick up 4 sts along second heel flap edge and k first 3 sts of heel. Place marker here for beg of next rnd.
- Work in rnds, adjusting so that there are 8 sts on each needle (24 sts total). Work 1 rnd even. On next rnd, decrease as follows: at end of needle 1, ssk. Repeat these 2 rnds until there are 16 sts. Work 2 rnds even or until foot measures ½" less than desired length.

- **Shape toe:** K 1 rnd even. Decrease on next rnd as follows: At end of needle 1, k last 2 sts tog. At beg of needle 2, ssk. At end of needle 2, k2tog. At beg of needle 3, ssk. Work 1 rnd even. Repeat these 2 rnds, dec 4 sts every other rnd, until there are 8 sts. Break yarn, leaving a 5" tail. Place sts of needles 1 and 3 on one needle. There should now be 4 sts each on two needles.
- Refer to Kitchener Stitch on page 122. Weave toe, using Kitchener st.

RUBY'S BUNNY LITTLE ROLL HAT

Hat

- Using spn and CC, CO 55 sts.
- Work in st st for 6 rows, following Ruby's Bunny Little Roll Hat Graph.
- Change to MC and continue in st st for 4 rows.
- To make holes for bunny ears: K18 sts, BO2 sts, k20 sts, BO2 sts, k18 sts (to end).
- On next row, CO where you BO, making 55 sts once again.
- K 1 row.
- Beg decreasing for the top:
    Row 1: *K8, k2tog* (6 times)
    Row 2: P

Row 3: *K7, k2tog* (6 times)
Row 4: P
Row 5: *K6, k2tog* (6 times)
Row 6: P2tog, p5
Row 7: *K4, k2tog* (6 times)
Row 8: P2tog, p3
Row 9: *K2, k2tog* (6 times)
Row 10: P2tog, p
Row 11: K2tog all around until there are 6 sts.

- Using yarn needle, draw these sts tog and tie off inside hat.

Finishing

- Seam back of hat, making certain to seam bottom 6 rows on the reverse side. This is so that when the brim is turned up the seam does not show.

Ruby's Bunny Little Roll Hat Graph

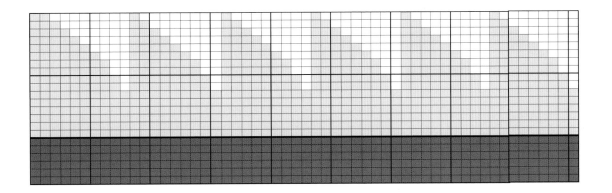

Sweet Grace

Materials

YARN

100% wool, handspun, sportweight

Any number of colors
(see graphs)

NOTIONS

Single-pointed knitting needles,
size 4, or size to obtain gauge

Yarn needle

MEASUREMENT

small, fits a 16" doll

GAUGE

6 sts x 8 rows = 1"

STITCH PATTERNS

St st, K1P1 ribbing

SWEET GRACE HEART SWEATER

Sweater Back

- Using spn and CC, CO 36 sts.
- Work in st st for 4 rows.
- Change to MC and work, following the Sweet Grace Heart Sweater Graph on page 109 for 43 rows.
- **Shape back of neck:** K10 sts, k2tog, k to within 11 sts of end, skp, and k10 sts. Put center 12 sts on a holder for back of neck.
- K 2 rows on left shoulder, then put these sts on a holder.
- On right side, change color and work in K1P1 ribbing for 4 rows for inside neck placket.
- BO.

Sweater Front

- Using spn and CC, CO 36 sts.
- Work in st st for 4 rows.
- Change to MC and work for 31 rows (including first 4 rows), following the graph.
- **Shape neck:** Put center 8 sts on a holder and work each side separately. Decrease on every other row four times at neck edge on each side. Remember to decrease 1 st in from the edge. For left slant, use skp; for

right slant, use k2tog. Use appropriate decrease for each side of the neck.

- Four rows before the top on the left side, change color and work in K1P1 ribbing, continuing to decrease at neck edge. After 2 rows, make a small buttonhole by BO 1 st halfway across the row and CO this st again, on the next row.
- BO this side and put the other side on holder.

Shoulders

- Match shoulder tog. K shoulder tog from inside.
- On left side, there will be a small placket with one buttonhole in front and a small placket to sew one button onto on the back. Sew small button on. This will allow a doll or animal with a large head to fit through sweater neck opening.

Sleeve

Note: On the left side (where your small placket is), overlap both plackets, just as they are when buttoned before picking up sts. The needle will go through both layers as if they were one when picking up this side.

- Pick up 30 sts, with 15 on either side of the shoulder—pick up 3 sts, skip 1 st, all along.
- Using MC, work in st st, decreasing on every eighth row three times until there are 24 sts.
- Work in st st for 6 more rows.
- Change to CC and work 4 more rows.
- BO loosely.
- Repeat for other sleeve.
- Sew sweater tog, matching underarm seams.

Neck

- Pick up 56 sts around the neck, starting at the shoulder placket and work back and forth for 4 rows.
- BO, leaving an opening where shoulder placket is.

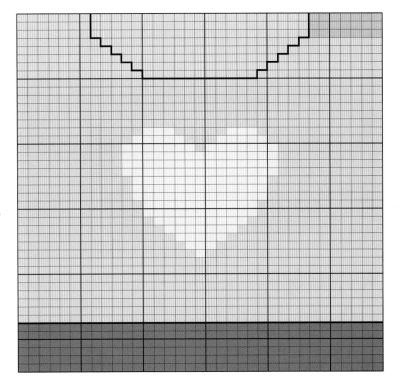

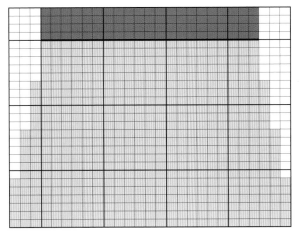

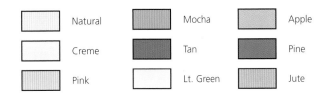

Natural   Mocha   Apple
Creme   Tan   Pine
Pink   Lt. Green   Jute

SWEET GRACE DOT SKIRT

Front and Back

(make two)

- Using spn and color of choice, CO 40 sts.
- Work in K1P1 ribbing for 4 rows.
- Work in st st, following Sweet Grace Dot Skirt Graph and decreasing on every fifth row until there are 28 sts.
- Work in K1P1 ribbing for 5 rows.
- BO.
- Sew front and back tog.
- Make a twisted string 20" long.
- Thread through skirt, over 3 sts and under 3 sts, starting at center front.

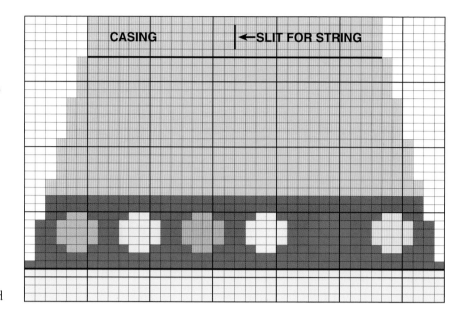

SWEET GRACE DOT SOCK

Sock

- Using spn and MC, CO 40 sts.
- Work in st st for 30 rows, following the Sweet Grace Dot Sock Graph, ending with a purl row.
- Continue in pattern and beg decrease, or shaping, for the toe of the sock.

    Row 1: K1, skp, k10, k2tog, skp, k10, k2tog, k1

    Row 2: P1, p2tog, p8, p2tog, p2tog, p8, p2tog, p1

    Row 3: K1, skp, k6, k2tog, skp k6, k2tog, k1

    Row 4: P1, p2tog, p4, p2tog, p2tog, p4, p2tog, p1 until there are 14 sts.

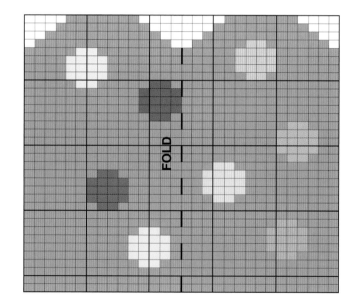

- Refer to Kitchener Stitch on page 122. At this point, fold sock in half and use Kitchener st to connect 7 sts to 7 sts on either side of sock.
- Seam sock tog.

Flower Scarf

Materials

YARN

100% wool, handspun, sportweight

MC - Mocha
CC (A) - Bark
CC (B) - Brick
CC (C) - Brown
CC (D) - Butter
CC (E) - Celery
CC (F) - Dk Brown
CC (G) - Dk Green
CC (H) - Gold
CC (I) - Pine

NOTIONS

Single-pointed knitting needles, size 4, or size to obtain gauge

Yarn needle

MEASUREMENTS

7" wide x 58" long

GAUGE

6 sts x 8 rows = 1"

STITCH PATTERNS

St st, Seed st

Scarf

- Using spn, CO 40 sts.
- Work in Seed st for 6 rows.
- Work length of scarf in st st, following the Flower Scarf Graph on pages 112–113, always starting and ending with 4 sts of Seed st in MC.
- Work in Seed st in MC for 6 rows.
- BO.

Finishing

- Make a 4" fringe in MC and attach to both ends of scarf.

Flower Scarf Graph SECTIONS 1 & 2

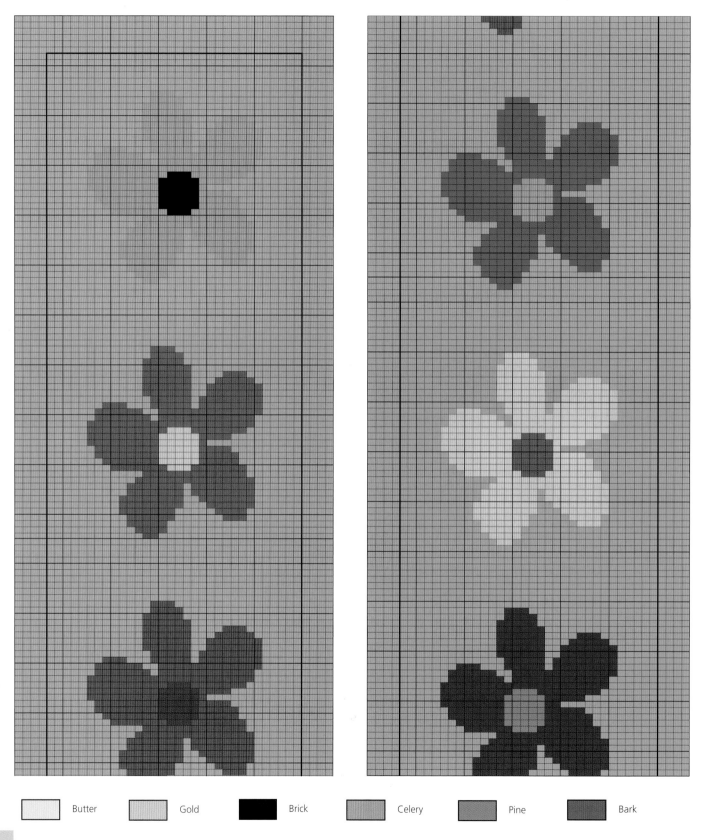

| | Butter | | Gold | | Brick | | Celery | | Pine | | Bark |

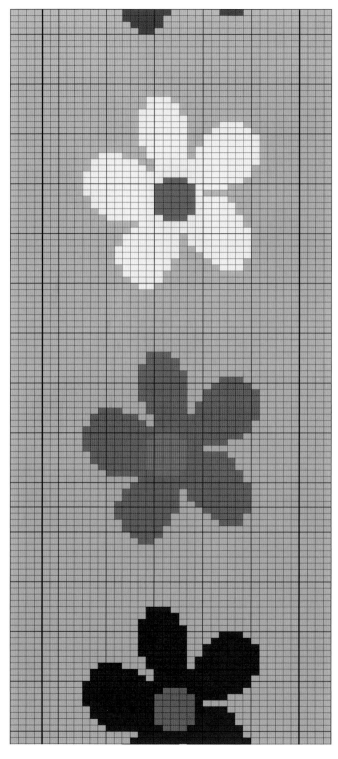

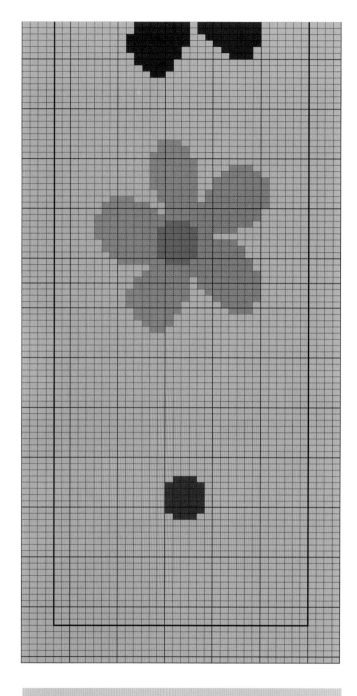

Dk. Green   Brown

Mocha   Dk. Brown

Color-photocopy the graph sections on these two pages. Piece the photocopies together with Section 1 at the top, then Section 2 followed by Section 3, and Section 4 at the bottom. Begin knitting at the bottom-right corner of the graph and work to the left and up.

Max and Franny Christmas Stockings

Materials

YARN

100% wool, handspun, sportweight

  for Max:

    MC – Violet
    CC (A) – Black
    CC (B) – Burgundy
    CC (C) – Charcoal
    CC (D) – Grape
    CC (E) – Indigo
    CC (F) – Lilac
    CC (G) – Purple
    CC (H) – Royal
    CC (I) – Silver

OR

  for Franny:

    MC – Celery
    CC (A) – Black
    CC (B) – Burgundy
    CC (C) – Charcoal
    CC (D) – Dk Brown
    CC (E) – Dk Green
    CC (F) – Grape
    CC (G) – Khaki
    CC (H) – Pine
    CC (I) – Purple
    CC (J) – Royal

NOTIONS

Circular knitting needles, size 4
Crochet hook, size E
Single-pointed knitting needles, size 4, or size to obtain gauge
Yarn needle

MEASUREMENT

28" long (from cuff to tip of toe)

GAUGE

6 sts x 8 rows = 1"

STITCH PATTERNS

St st, K1P1 ribbing

Leg

- Using spn and MC, loosely CO 80 sts.
- Work in K1P1 ribbing for 25 rows, following Max Christmas Stocking Graph on pages 118–119 or Franny Christmas Stocking Graph on pages 120–121.
- Change to st st and work until you reach the heel (approximately 16").

Heel

- Transfer all sts onto circular needle.
- Seam back of sock.
- Break yarn.
- Put center 40 sts on holder.
- Work back and forth on heel flap, 20 sts on either side of seam.
- Join the yarn, on the knit side, working back and forth on the back 40 sts in MC as follows:
- Work first 4 sts and last 4 sts in garter st and the center 32 sts in st st for 26 rows.
- End with a knit row.

- **Turn heel**: Work short rows as follows:

    Row 1: P22, p2tog, p1 turn work

    Row 2: Sl 1, k5, k2tog, k1 turn

    Row 3: Sl 1, p6, p2tog, p1 turn

    Row 4: Sl 1, k7, k2tog, k1 turn

    Row 5: Sl 1, p8, p2tog, p1 turn

    Row 6: Sl 1, k9, k2tog, k1 turn

    Row 7: Sl 1, p10, p2tog, p1 turn

    Row 8: Sl 1, k11, k2tog, k1 turn

    Row 9: Sl 1, p12, p2tog, p1 turn

    Row 10: Sl 1, k13, k2tog, k1 turn

    Row 11: Sl 1, p14, p2tog, p1 turn

    Row 12: Sl 1, k15, k2tog, k1 turn

    Row 13: Sl 1, p16, p2tog, p1 turn

    Row 14: Sl 1, k17, k2tog, k to the end of the row until there are 26 sts.
- Break yarn.
- Put these 26 sts on a holder.
- With circular needle, on the RS of work, pick up and k 26 sts along the left side of the heel flap.
- K across the 26 sts that are on the holder.
- Pick up and k 26 sts along the RS of the heel flap.
- K following the graph across the 40 sts of the instep until there are 118 sts.
- P back.

Note: The pattern should be uninterrupted from the calf onto the foot.

- **Shape gusset:** Work back and forth across all 118 sts, decreasing 1 st on both sides of the patterned instep until 80 sts remain.
- The work will now be open on the side and will be worked back and forth on the circular needle now because of the shape of the stocking.

Note: The bottom of the sock is worked solid in MC, while the top of the sock continues in the design as detailed on the graph.

- K for 6½".
- End with a purl row.
- **Shape toe:**

    Rnd 1: K1, k2tog, k34, k2tog, k2, k2tog, k34, k2tog, k1

    Rnd 2: P1, p2tog, p32, p2tog, p2, p2tog, p32, p2tog, p1

    Rnd 3: K1, k2tog, k30, k2tog, k2, k2tog, k30, k2tog, k1

    Rnd 4: P1, p2tog, p28, p2tog, p2, p2tog, p28, p2tog, p1

    Rnd 5: K1, k2tog, k26, k2tog, k2, k2tog, k26, k2tog, k1

    Rnd 6: P1, p2tog, p24, p2tog, p2, p2tog, p24, p2tog, p1

    Rnd 7: K1, k2tog, k22, k2tog, k2, k2tog, k22, k2tog, k1

    Rnd 8: P1, p2tog, p20, p2tog, p2, p2tog, p20, p2tog, p1

    Rnd 9: K1, k2tog, k18, k2tog, k2, k2tog, k18, k2tog, k1

    Rnd 10: P1, p2tog, p16, p2tog, p2, p2tog, p16, p2tog, p1

    Rnd 11: K1, k2tog, k14, k2tog, k2, k2tog, k14, k2tog, k1until there are 32 sts.
- Turn work to the purl side.
- Put 16 sts on one spn and 16 sts on another.
- K the two sides tog.

Finishing

- Seam up the side.
- Fold the cuff in half.
- Using crochet hook, make a crocheted loop to the desired length in MC.
- Attach loop onto top edge of stocking.

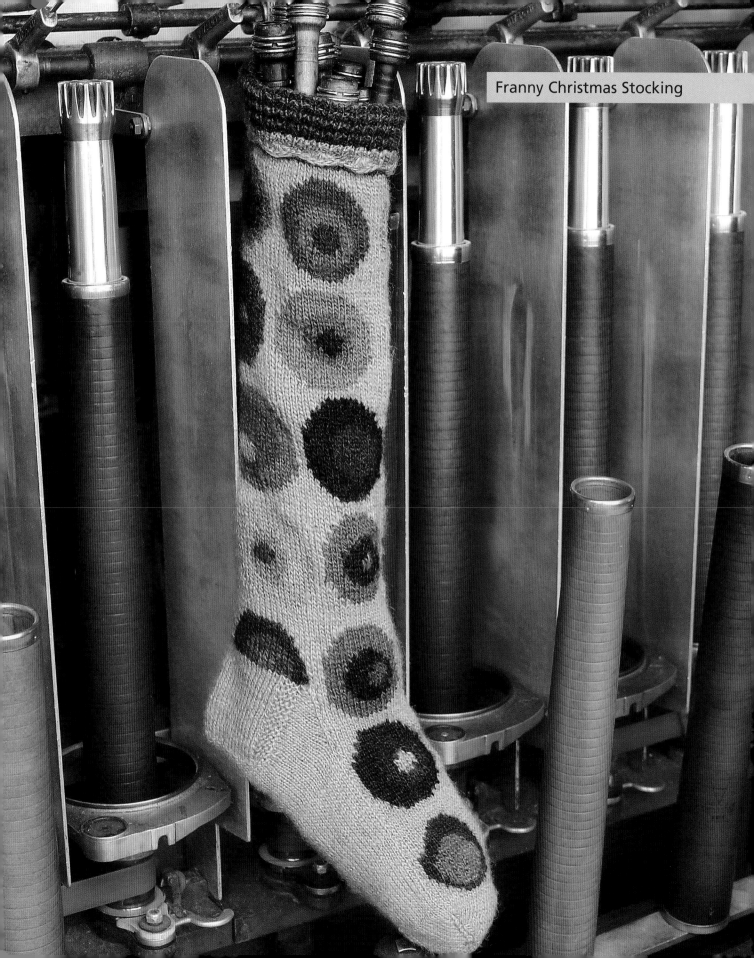

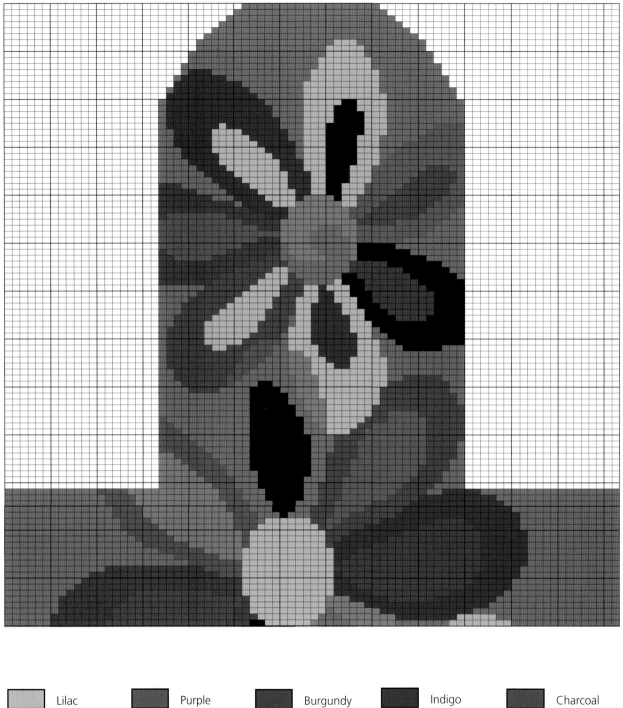

	Lilac		Purple		Burgundy		Indigo		Charcoal
	Grape		Violet		Royal		Silver		Black

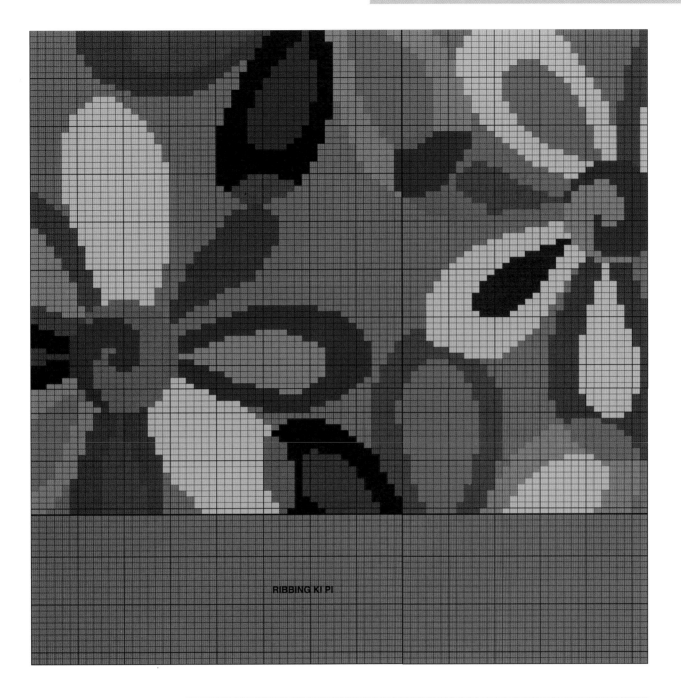

RIBBING K1 P1

Color-photocopy the graph sections. Piece the photocopies together with Section 1 at the top, and Section 2 at the bottom. Begin knitting at the bottom-right corner of the graph and work to the left and up.

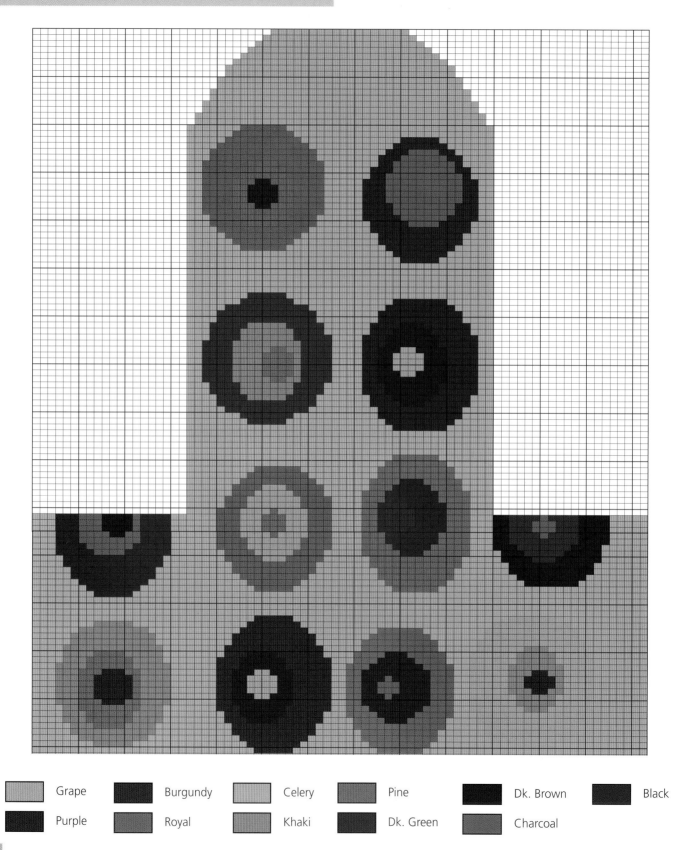

	Grape		Burgundy		Celery		Pine		Dk. Brown		Black
	Purple		Royal		Khaki		Dk. Green		Charcoal		

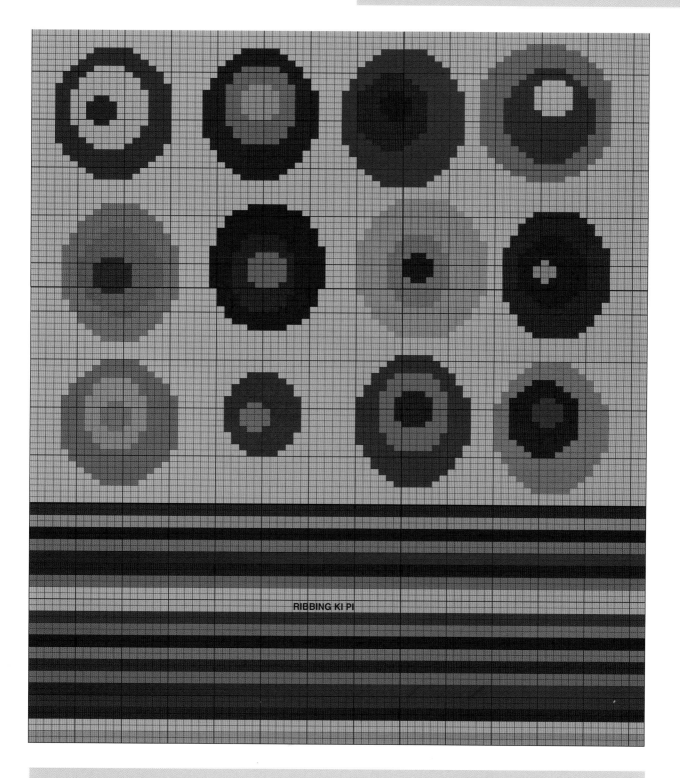

RIBBING K1 P1

Color-photocopy the graph sections. Piece the photocopies together with Section 1 at the top, and Section 2 at the bottom. Begin knitting at the bottom-right corner of the graph and work to the left and up.

Stitch Glossary

BULLION ROSE

1. Come up at A and go down at B, leaving a loop. (See Fig. 1)
2. Come up again at A with the needle tip only. Wrap the loop thread around the needle tip until the twists equal the distance between A and B. (See Fig. 2)
3. Draw the needle through the twists and gently pull the thread through; as you pull the thread, hold the twists flat on the surface with the needle. (See Fig. 3)
4. Go down again at B and pull firmly to secure the knot. (See Fig. 4)

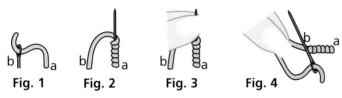

Fig. 1   **Fig. 2**   **Fig. 3**   **Fig. 4**

CORKSCREW FRINGE

- Using spn and MC, CO 75 sts.
   Row 1: *K1f&b and k1* (in each st, creating 3 sts out of each one)
   Row 2: BO all sts purlwise.
- Repeat for indicated pieces of corkscrew fringe.
- Use your fingers to twist each tassel into a corkscrew.
- Attach corkscrew fringe as indicated in project instructions.

CROCHETED FLOWER

Using crochet hook, chain 3 sts and connect to make a circle by slipping the last st into the first st. Make 2 SC into each chain from the previous circle. Continue in this manner until flower center is 14 sts. Complete 3 rnds without increasing. On the next rnd, make 3 TrC into every other SC. On the next rnd, make 3 TrC into every st.

GARTER STITCH

- Knit every row.

INTARSIA

- Wind as many bobbins as necessary for desired pattern. Work from the bobbins rather than the whole ball of yarn.
- Start at bottom-right corner of graph and work left on first (RS) row, changing yarn colors as directed. Place the "old" color of yarn over the "new" color of yarn at the back of the knitted piece and continue working with the "new" color. (See Fig. 1)
- Work next (WS) row to the right. Place the "new" color yarn over the "old" color yarn at the front of the knitted piece and continue working with the "new" color. (See Fig. 2)

Note: On the back of the work, a two-color chain forms where the yarns cross.

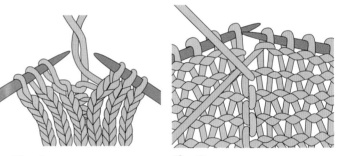

Fig. 1   **Fig. 2**

KITCHENER STITCH

This technique is also called grafting or weaving. It is a way to join two pieces of knitting invisibly. Abut two sets of sts, still on their needles, tog with RSs up. Thread a strand of matching yarn about four times as long as the join on a yarn needle. Beginning at the right edge, follow this sequence:

a. Bring the yarn needle through the front st as if to p, leaving the st on the knitting needle.
b. Bring the yarn needle through the back st as if to k, leaving the st on the needle.
c. Bring the yarn needle through the same front st as if to k, then sl this st off the needle. Bring the yarn needle through the next front st as if to p, again leaving the st on the needle.

d. Bring the yarn needle through the first back st as if to p, sl that st off, then bring the yarn needle through the next back st as if to k, leaving it on the needle.

Repeat C and D until all sts have been worked. The yarn needle will enter each st twice, one knitwise and once purlwise. You can adjust the tension on this row after all sts have been worked.

(See Fig. 1)

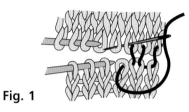

Fig. 1

KNITTED CORD

- Using dpn, CO 3 sts.

- ★K3★ Do not turn work, slide sts to right end of needle. Pull yarn to tighten. Repeat from ★ to ★ until cord measures 34".

- K all 3 sts tog and pull yarn through last st.

KNITTED LEAF

- Using spn and color B, CO 5 sts.
    Row 1: (RS): K2, yo, k1, yo, k2 = 7 sts
    Row 2 (and all even rows): P
    Row 3: K3, yo, k1, yo, k3 = 9 sts
    Row 5: K4, yo, k1, yo, k4 = 11 sts
    Row 7: Ssk, k7, k2tog = 9 sts
    Row 9: Ssk, k5, k2tog = 7 sts
    Row 11: Ssk, k3, k2tog = 5 sts
    Row 13: Ssk, k1, k2tog = 3 sts
    Row 15: Sl 1, k2tog, psso = 1 st.

- BO.

KNITTED ROSE

- Using spn and color A, CO 2 sts.

- Working in st st, increase 1 st on one edge only, every other row, until there are 17 sts. You will now have one curved edge.

- Work in st st for 2".

- Decrease 1 st every other row on the same side as the increases until there is 1 st.

- Pull yarn through this last st and leave a long end, approximately 18". The piece will now be shaped on one side and straight on the other side.

- Place the piece flat on work surface with the knit side facing up, the shaped side on the bottom, and the straight edge on the top.

- On the right side, fold 1" in on itself, then roll the folded edge loosely toward the other end until it is all rolled up.

- Make certain to keep the shaped edge lined up and the other edge (the straight edge) will curve down to make a nice rose shape.

- Using yarn needle and long end, secure the base of the rose.

LAZY DAISY

1. Come up at A and form a loop. (See Fig. 1)

2. Go down at B (as close to A as possible, but not into it) and emerge at C, bringing the needle tip over the loop. (See Fig. 2)

3. Go down at D, making a smaller anchor stitch. (See Fig. 3)

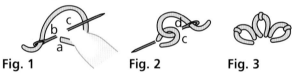

Fig. 1   **Fig. 2**   **Fig. 3**

POM-POM

1. Using craft scissors, cut two 2¾" circles with a ¾" hole in the center from cardboard. Place them together to form a disk. (See Fig. 1)

Fig. 1

2. Double a long strand of yarn on a yarn needle. Take the needle through the hole, wrap the yarn around outside edge of the disk, and through the hole again. Continue until the entire disk is covered and the hole is nearly filled. (See Fig. 2)

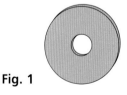

Fig. 2

3. Insert the point of sharp scissors between the two disks at their outer edge and cut the yarn all around. Spread the disks apart slightly. Tightly tie a doubled length of yarn around the center of the yarn between the disks and knot securely. (See Fig. 3)

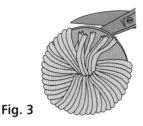

Fig. 3

4. Cut through each disk and remove from yarn. Trim all around the yarn ball (except for the tie yarn lengths) to make it as even as possible.

STOCKINETTE STITCH

- K on the RS and p on the WS.

TASSEL

1. Cut a piece of cardboard 4" wide by the desired length of the tassel plus 1" for tying and trimming. Wrap yarn 40 times (or to desired thickness) around length of cardboard. Cut a piece of yarn about 18" long and thread, doubled, onto yarn needle. Insert needle under all strands at upper edge of cardboard. Pull tightly and knot securely near strands. (See Fig. 1)

2. Cut yarn loops at edge of cardboard.

3. Cut a piece of yarn 12" long and wrap tightly around loops, 1½" below top knot to form tassel neck. Knot securely, thread ends onto yarn needle and pull ends to center of tassel. Trim tassel ends evenly. (See Fig. 2)

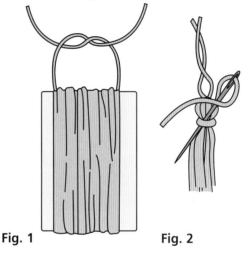

Fig. 1   **Fig. 2**

Knitting Abbreviations

beg	begin(ning)	rnd	round	
BO	bind off	rs	right side	
CC	contrast color	Seed st	seed stitch	
CO	cast on	skp	slip 1, knit 1, pass slipped	
dpn	double-pointed knitting needles	sl	slip	
		spn	single-pointed, or straight, knitting needles	
garter st	garter stitch			
k	knit(ting)	ssk	slip 1 stitch as if to knit, slip another stitch as if to knit, then knit these 2 stitches together	
K1f&b	knit 1 stitch on the front and 1 stitch in the back			
K1P1	ribbing knit 1, purl 1 to create ribbing	st	stitch	
		st st	stockinette stitch	
k2tog	knit 2 stitches together	tbl	through back loop(s)	
MC	main color	tog	together	
p	purl	ws	wrong side	
p2tog	purl 2 stitches together	yo	yarn over	
rem	remain(ing)(s)			

Crochet Abbreviations

DC	double crochet
SC	single crochet
TrC	triple crochet

About the Authors

Twenty years ago, Andrea Shackleton and Gayle Shackleton, sisters from Northern California, started designing and knitting sweaters by hand. With a love of fine art, heirloom knitting, crochet, and antique buttons and trims, they create one-of-a-kind pieces for private collections and galleries. Andrea and Gayle design both Hot Knots and Tara sweaters, with their line including not only handknits but also fine dresses, accessories, and children's sweaters.

In 1990, through Aid to Artisans, Andrea and Gayle were given the rare opportunity to help a women's knitting cooperative in Nepal. Now, more than 14 years later, they are still working with the wonderful women of the Association of Craft Producers, a nonprofit women's cooperative in Katmandu, Nepal. ACP dyes all of the yarn for Tara sweaters with technology that is clean and nonpolluting. The Tara sweaters are also handknit by ACP. As a result of the joint effort, the women in the cooperative now own their own studios. Increased wages, retirement programs, health care, and educational scholarships are a few of the benefits available to those involved.

"Working with ACP has been one of the richest experiences of our lives," says Gayle. "Named for the Nepali Goddess of compassion, 'Tara' represents our ever-expanding collaboration."

At home in Arcata, California, where Hot Knots is based, a small group of talented women work together to create fine pieces of wearable art. In recent years, Andrea and Gayle have also opened a store in this little gold rush town. They have found it to be a great new source of creativity and inspiration.

Andrea and Gayle have four children between them, ages 3 through 9. Their love of fun and unlimited creativity are a constant source of inspiration. "They are the best things we ever made."

Dedication

We would like to dedicate this book to our mom, Ann Shackleton, who taught us the love of making beautiful things.

Acknowledgments

Great thanks and love to Jeff DeMark, Jeff Belton, Alice, Hannah, Jesse, and Sophia, whose presence in our lives is what makes it all worth it.

About the Site of the Photography

In 1871, Baron Woolen Mills opened as part of a cooperative venture of the Church of Jesus Christ of Latter-day Saints and its members in Brigham City, Utah.

Originally built in 1869–1870, the mill was one of several businesses added into the Brigham City Mercantile and Manufacturing Association, established by Lorenzo Snow, then apostle of the church, who oversaw the settlement of the Mormon community.

The mill—the only one of its kind west of the Mississippi—provided a full-process operation. It purchased wool fleece from local sheep ranchers; then the raw material was cleaned, dyed, carded, spun, woven, and finished—all on site. By 1877, the mill had 200 spindles and seven looms, and was producing $42,000 worth of woolen products in 44 weeks. It would later burn down, be rebuilt, burn again, and rise once more to become the employer of the largest direct sales force in the United States in the early 1930s, managing the efforts of some 700 people.

The mill gained its name through four generations of ownership by the Baron family. Since the Baron family's departure, the mill experienced one, short-lived ownership that ended in bankruptcy, and then a period of revival in the 1990s.

Today it is a quiet, mostly abandoned spot where photographers gather to record intriguing images of the vintage machinery that fills the old stone and brick building.

Because the mill is highly prized both for its historical significance and for its artistic imagery, the current owners are working to breath new life into the structure and save it from being demolished.

This work includes a plan to move some of the equipment to a single area of the mill where they would put together a two-section living history museum. One section would be dedicated to the 1930s era of the mill—the time period from which much of the operating machinery came—while the other section would highlight the operation as it was in the 1870s.

Another idea is to build a small restaurant in the back area and turn the upper floor into a reception center and conference area—all while retaining the historic look and feel of the mill.

If you would like to know more about Baron Woolen Mills, go to www.baronwoolenmills.com on the Internet.

Yarn Amounts

The yarn we use has an approximate yardage of 70 yards per ounce. If your yarn differs in yardage, then account for that by using more or less weight of yarn. *Note: Greater yardage would equal less weight used, less yardage per ounce would require more weight of yarn.*

Circles Scarf, *page 10*
MC: 8 oz.
10 CC: 1 oz each

Circles Hat, *page 14*
MC: 4 oz.
10 CC: .25 oz. each

Dot Glove, *page 18*
MC: 4 oz.
4 CC: .25 oz. each

Dot Hat, *page 20*
MC: 4 oz.
10 CC: .25–.5 oz. each

Dot Sweater, *page 23*
MC: 28 oz.
11 CC: .5 oz. each

Cherry Blossom Mitten, *page 34*
MC: 4 oz.
4 CC: .25–.5 oz. each

Cherry Blossom Scarf, *page 37*
MC: 16 oz.
CC (F) trim color: 4 oz.
6 CC: 2 oz. each (depending on size of pom poms)

Ruffle-edged Glove, *page 40*
MC: 4 oz.
CC (A): .5 oz.
CC (B): 10–20 yds.

Ruffle-edged Pillbox Hat, *page 43*
MC: 4 oz.
CC (A): .5 oz.
CC (B): 10–20 yds.

Ruffle-edged Drawstring Bag, *page 44*
MC: 6 oz.
CC (A): .5 oz.
CC (B): 10–20 yds.

Rose Hat, *page 46*
MC: 4 oz.
CC (A): .5 oz.
CC (B): .5 oz.

Rose Scarf, *page 48*
MC: 16 oz.
CC (A): .5 oz.
CC (B): .5 oz.

Big Squares Knee Sock, *page 50*
MC: 8 oz.
8 CC: .5 oz. each

Painted Flower Fingerless Mitten, *page 54*
Combined weight of all yarns: 3 oz.

Painted Flower Hat, *page 56*
Combined weight of all yarns: 4 oz.

Painted Flower Scarf, *page 57*
Combined weight of all yarns: 16 oz.

Pablo Bag, *page 58*
8 colors: 1 oz. each
Strap color: 2 oz.

Ribbed Market Bag, *page 62*
7 colors: 2 oz. each

Ribbed Scarf, *page 68*
9 colors: 2 oz. each

Ribbed Hat, *page 69*
6 colors: 1 oz. each

Jesse's Topknot Hat, *page 78*
11 colors: .5 oz. each

Jesse's Cardigan, *page 82*
11 colors: 1–1.5 oz. each color (depending on size)

Striped Mitten, *page 90*
Combined weight of all yarns: 4 oz.

Companion Topknot Hat, *page 92*
Combined weight of all yarns: 4 oz.

Ruby's Daisy Hat, *page 94*
MC: 3 oz.
Trim colors: 10–20 yds. each

Ruby's Daisy Sweater, *page 96*
MC: 12–16 oz. (depending on size)
CC (D): 2 oz.
CC (B): 1 oz.
CC (A) & (C): .5 oz. each

Flower Scarf, *page 111*
MC: 12 oz.
9 CC: .5 oz. each

Max and Franny Christmas Stockings, *page 114*
MC: 4 oz.
9 CC: .5 oz. each

Index